NAIMISHA

NAIMISHA-GARUDA PURANAM

T.KRISHNA DINESH

I would like to thank everyone.

Who are sincerely book lovers?

My family and friends.

Finally to my caring, supporting and loving parents my deepest gratitude.

Your encouragement when the time is tough is much appreciated and duly noticed.

MY Heartful thanks.

Contents

Contents

FOREWORD

To The book lovers,

I hope this book helps you to get you out of your work and take you to the world of love.

I would love nothing more than seeing the book in your hands everywhere –Readers walking down the streets, the browser's in a book store, at home.

That's a great challenge which lies ahead of me but it is certainly worth an attempt.

Take out time from your busy schedule to rejoice.

Hope you read and Enjoy.

PREFACE

The *Garuda Purana* is one of 18 Mahāpurāṇa texts in Hinduism.

It is a part of Vaishnavism literature corpus, primarily centering around Hindu god Vishnu.

It is in the form of a dialog between Vishnu and Garuda, the King of Birds.

The second section of this Purana (given here) deals with issues connected with death, particularly funeral rites and the metaphysics of reincarnation.

Suuthamuni told this purana to Naimacharanya munis and his students.

This book cane be ready by everyone at any time it is a Mahapurana one who read or listen this get Maha Punya.

ACKNOWLEDGEMENTS

"I would like to take this opportunity to thank my publishing team."

"Thanks to everyone on the Book in the team who helped me so much".

I cannot express enough thanks to my book team for their continued support.

I offer my sincere appreciation for the learning and opportunity

I
Introduction

WHAT IS THE CAUSE OF THE BIRTH AND DEATH OF LIVING BEINGS IN THIS WORLD?

AFTER TAKING BIRTH AND EXPERIENCING A PROPER LIFE, LATER DUE TO WHAT ACTIONS A BEING ATTAINS SWARGA AND NARAKA (HEAVEN AND HELL)?

DUE TO WHAT REASON DO INCURABLE DISEASES COME ABOUT?

WHEN A BEING GETS CONVERTED TO BHUTA, PRETHA AND PISASU, LIKE FORMLESS BEINGS?

HOW TO GET MUKTHI OR MOKSHA FROM THE CYCLE OF BIRTH AND DEATH?

THUS ASKED THE EXALTED RESIDENTS OF NAIMICHARANYA TO MUNI SUUTHA

THIS IS A TALE OF PATH, JIVES TAKE AFTER LIFE IN THIS WORLD

Introduction of Yama :

Yama, the God of death was the son of Surya, the sun God and Saranya, the daughter of Vishvakarma. He is the twin brother of Yami, who became the river Yamuna.

He was the first mortal to die and so, was made the God of death. His noose is always following everybody and it is the distance between the noose and people that decides their life. Yama along with his accountant Chitragupta keeps count of everybody's deeds. If a person performs good deeds he goes to heaven, bad deeds to hell and if both, then back to earth for another life.

On Yama's death, his twin Yami could not be consoled and hence the Gods created night and day and the cycle of time began.

Initially, Yama was very good looking but due to it, he was never concentrating on his work. Bad deeds increased in the world as there was no fear of death. So Lord Shiva cursed him to lose his good looks. Hence Yama became green-skinned, wearing red clothes and riding a buffalo.

Yama's wives are Dhumorna, who is the goddess of the funeral pyre and Vijaya, the daughter of a Brahmin.

Yama had asked Vijaya not to go to a particular section of *patala* but when she went there ignoring his command, she saw her own mother chained and suffering.

Yama refused to let her mother go unless there was a replacement and she was released only when an old woman took her place.

Hence the story of Yama teaches us to do good deeds always and to never bend the rules whoever might be asking for it.

Yama is said to have been the first mortal who died. By virtue of precedence, he became the ruler of the departed and therefore the lord and judge of the dead.

The Devatas are the wise entities of the heaven and Yama is one of the wisest of all. Yama is also referred as Dharma because he is believed to be the lord of justice. He is dedicated towards maintaining order and harmony.

He is the Yamraj is the ruler of the hell.

However, in the Vedic times, the conception of hell had not fully developed. Yama is the god of death and holds charge of the several hells mentioned in the Puranas.

Naraka in Hinduism serves only as a temporary purgatory where the soul is purified of sin by its suffering. Naraka holds many hells, and Yama directs departed souls to the appropriate one. Even elevated Mukti-yogyas and Nitya-samsarins can experience Naraka for expiation of Papa karma.

Although Yama is the lord of Naraka, he may also direct the soul to a Swarga (heaven) or return it to Bhoomi (earth). As good and bad deeds are not considered to cancel each other out, the same soul may spend time in both a hell and a heaven. The seven Swargas are: Bhuvas, Swas (governed by Indra), Tharus, Thaarus, Savithaa, Prapithaa, Maha (governed by Brahma).

NON COVETNESS IS THE HAPPY LIFE

Lord Brahma came out of the navel of Lord Vishnu. He is the creator of this entire universe. In this wide beautiful world created by Lord Brahma there is a holy place called Naimicharanyam surrounded by dense forests.

In that place dwelt the great sage Sownaka and his disciples. The place being serene and ideal for doing penance and other austerities, the place always held attraction for Veda pandits, singers of Harikatha and other holy souls.

To such a place Muni Suutha, the great disciple of renowned Veda vyasa was going. As soon as Sownaka and disciples spotted him they went forward with great enthusiasm and welcomed Suutha Muni with warmth. They made him sit on an exalted high seat with respect and surrounded him giving their pranams.

Then sage Sownaka addressed the great soul Suutha, `Oh! Learned Muni, we have listened from you the Vaisnva and Shaiva puranas. We understand the puranas of Lord Brahma are filled with raja guna, the puranas of Lord Shiva are filled with tamasa guna while the puranas of Lord Vishnu are filled with satva guna.

Now we kindly request you to tell us a puranas of Lord Vishnu. We are very eager to hear your words of wisdom. You are the disciple of the great sage Vedavyasa who is considered to be incarnation of Lord Vishnu himself.

He himself has preached you everything. There is nothing you are not aware. You must kindly tell us a satvic purana which will give us the four purushartha namely dharma, wealth, happiness and house. This is only our wish and request.

Oh! Great muni in this world why living things take birth and later die?

A person born in this world and living a full life, due to which actions reaches heaven and hell?

Due to which reason a person get affected by disease from which there is no cure?

When a person gets ghost (pretha) form?

How such a form and state will come to an end? How he will get mukti and release from bondage?

Please tell all these clearly in a way we understand

Thus the assembled learned ones asked with great humility to Muni Suutha.

Seeing their earnest faces Muni Suutha with great compassion meditated on his guru Vyasa maharishi, raised his hand and did pranams to Lord Narayana who is the cause and protector of the entire world.

Then addressing Sownaka and the others, he told `Oh! Exalted Brahmins: men who are great tapasinis, good souls who are aware of many things, you asked me a good question.

As an answer to these questions, I will tell you a good purana listen to this with full concentration.

Once the king of birds Garuda asked a similar question for the welfare of this world to Lord Sriman Narayana, who is the all-knowing seer who is the creator, protector and destroyer of this entire universe, who is the Purushothaman of this world.

Lord answered Garuda in a proper manner and made him understand the answers for these questions. I will tell you the conversation as it happened between Lord Narayana and king of birds Garuda. Listening to that will give you answers for all your riddles.

The king of birds Garuda addressed Lord Narayana, the Paramatma Oh! Jaganatha! Oh! Pranadhama, like oil hidden in the seed, you are hidden in all atmas, the param thing which is filled everywhere, Oh! Sri Hari tell me,

Why jives are born in this world?

After their death why they reach svarga and naraka?

Due to what sin jives after death get the Pretha or ghost form? By doing what punya that forms will be rid of?

By doing what karma's they will reach the world of Devas?

How to get rid of he previous sins before the death and reach a good state after death?

By doing what karmas the papas will get cleared.

At the time of death by thinking whom good state can be obtained?

You must kindly tell all these to your lowly servant and bless me.'

Thus entreated Garuda to Sriman Narayana.

Sriman narayana murthy, the all-knowing seer who enter into everybody's mind and can oversee everything, the purushotham who is the cause for all acts by every soul, Sri Hari Bhagawan smiled benevolently at the king of birds Garuda and started telling.

` Garuda you have asked a good question. Whatever you have asked are the secrets not known to the people of this world. A person who may live for however long soill it is definite he has to die.

This basic truth is not thought of by ordinary mortals. It is only one in million who thinks gravely that as birth, death is also an undeniable truth. Only a person who is keenly aware of the fact that at the end of this life one has to get caught by Yama dharma will think of proper ways of spending this life.

He will tend to think then, yesterday has gone, today is also getting over, as the days are getting over this life is getting exhausted without doing any good deeds. If Lord Yama comes tomorrow itself what will happen to my fate, thus thinking at least in fear he will try to do good dharmic deeds and try to live a life honestly.

If a person does good karmas during his lifetime, that karma itself will save him. Garuda it is written in Vedas and shashtras what karma each one has to do as per his birth and community in which he is born.

Realizing his dharmic position, if a person does properly the karmas entitled to him by birth in a particular sect not over reaching or going below his dharmic position, he alone will reach the correct place.

There are four varnas of people Brahmins, Khastriyas, vaishyas and shudras.

In that for Brahmins learning, to teach the learned texts, vethal, vetpithal, to give charity, to accept charity thus six karmas are binding to them.

For Kshatriya learning, vettal, iidhal, ulakombal, to learn about warfare, poruthal, thus six karmas are binding to them.

For Vaishyas learning, vettal, to collect property, iidhal, to take care of live stock, oill the land, thus six karmas are binding to them.

For shudras oothdhal, to work for the other communities, to collect money for living process, to take care of livestock, to oill the land, vettal these six karmas are binding to them.

The biggest penance of living is to follow one's discipline as destined by birth. Only such people will realize their yoga and get bhogas at the same time, live for long time and finally will reach their destined worlds.

Hence it is best for each one to follow one's discipline and do one's karmas properly as ordained.

It is not proper to covet for any wealth. Such longing for things and situations not ordained to one will cause downfall of one's position in life.

The wisdom is to leave the longings and covertness for things and live a peaceful life, thus Lord preached and blessed Garuda with his golden words of wisdom.

II

GOOD BIRTH AND THREE WISHES

Garuda the king of the birds was listening keenly to the words of Sriman Narayana. Then Lord Vasudeva further started telling to Garuda.

Oh! King of the birds! In this world there are 84 lakh living species. Their origin is in four ways. About 21 lakh species like have come from eggs like birds. About 21 lakh species have come from earth like trees and plants.

About 21 lakh species have come from fetus growing in bags like human beings and other mammals. About 21 lakh species have come from sweat like worms and insects.

Garuda it is most difficult to get human birth among all these births. This human birth is most sacred of all births. There are eyes to see things, ears to hear, tongue to taste different tastes, nose to smell many smells and sense to differentiate good and bad.

Holding these it is the human birth that is most exalted. In that human birth there are Brahmins, kshatriyas, vaisikas and Sudra, thus four sects of people.

The washer man who washes others clothes, the tanner who works on skin of animals, the dancer who entertains, the boat man who drives boat, the hunter all belong to sudra community.

Eating, sleeping, fear, sex these are common to all living beings. However wisdom is not common to all.

In whichever the land the black buks called `krishnacharam' are present that is a sacred land. In that land people who worship devas, munis and ancestors will augur lot of good things. In that punya boomi 33 crore devas bless the land with their presence.

Garuda, the booth and preth do not have any form. They are considered to be gaseous. In compared to them the jives who take life form as animals and birds and live with some sense are better life forms.

In comparison to them human life is soill better form. Among the humans too a Brahmin life soill exalted. Among the Brahmin persons, the one who are involved in the studies of Vedas and understanding of the puranas lead a better life in comparison to one's leading mundane lives getting embroiled in day to day living and squabbles.

More better lives are led by the ones who live steady lives along the path led by scriptures and the most exalted lives are led by persons who have realized Brahma gyan by leading dharmic life.

Among the crores of birth living beings get, it is the human birth which leads to swarga and getting mukthi. After getting such a human birth instead of doing good karmas and reach a good state, if one does bad karmas and reach the world of hell he is only but wasting the precious birth.

However such kind of people is more in this world. Such persons can be considered to be doing harm to oneself. Desire for land, women and wealth are three desires which lull the jive to do wrong things, go against one's own conscience and make them do evil things against other human interests , make him do adharma.

Such a person can be equalled to animal and can no more be counted as a co-human. The desires will lead to greed making the man turn away from feeling of love, wisdom and dharma.

Once a person is caught by desire and greed then his needs know no limit. He will run with insatiate feeling of more I want, what I have is not enough and will not settle to enjoy what he has and be satisfied.

Such a person if he gets 100 gold coins he will desire for 1000 gold coins. To obtain that he will not mind-crossing rules of what is right. Once he gets 1000 gold coins his desire will more to a lakh and crore gold coins.

Then he may like to make a country's part as his property. He will want to become the king and chakravathi or absolute ruler for the entire earth. Even after that the desires won't leave him. He would wish to become deva and king of devas, the Devendran thus desires have a way of multiplying as it gets fulfilled.

Staring with a desire to own a thing will change to a desire to own a land and from there to own women and wealth. As these desires grow in mind he gradually will loose human feelings of integrity, sincerity, love, brotherhood etc.

In confusion, with excess of desires the wisdom takes a back seat. On fulfilling one's desire he becomes selfish and works only for self-interest. He gradually starts along doing wrong to others and operates with the goal of just fulfilling his desires.

As his desires grow so his life span does not grow. A person who dies not annihilating such desires in the bud will loose his righteousness and become servile to others in order to get his desires fulfilled. He will start getting ridiculed by others. Finally after death will be pushed to hell.

To tumble and fall in a lowly path the main reason is the unchecked desires or covertness growing in the mind.

However the wise men who preach desire is the root cause of all evil and live a life of renunciation will reach swarga loka as they pass from his world Only a person who controls his senses and does not allow the mind to go the way of senses, lives an independent life and augurs all good.

A person in young age not heading to the advises of his parents during youth falls prey to attractions of beautiful women and tries to full fill her orders against what is right, in old age he may be humiliated by one's own progeny.

who may abandon him calling him old dependent soul.', hearing such harsh words he may be shattered, Thus it is more important in life to cultivate wisdom of self rather than collecting unwanted knowledge and studies.

Garuda! There are many ways by which the various senses like sense of touch, sense of taste, sense of smell can destroy one. Examples are many.

A spotted dear may hear a sweet music of the flute and may get engrossed in it leaving its caution about the hunters and may get caught. Thus its downfall is due to attraction of sense of hearing A male elephant caught by the attraction to a female elephant may follow it blindly only to fall into the pit laid by the elephant catcher. Thus here is the case of reaching one's end by sense of attraction.

As insects during rainy season get attracted to a burning lamp in the night thinking it to be a ripe fruit and fall in he burning lamp and give off their life. Here is a case of reaching one's end by attraction of sense of sight.

The honeybees with great attraction to the taste of honey collect them meticulously in their beehives. The hunters of honey too get attracted by the honey and kill and burn the hive and bees to collect honey. So here is a case of meeting one's end by sense of taste.

The fishes get attracted to the smell of the earthworm hung in
the hook and in turn get caught in the hook to meet their end. Here is a case of reaching one's end by sense of smell

Thus the attraction to different senses causes the downfall of various living being. This being so, the human beings endowed with five senses will have an attraction much greater than the other living beings. There is no doubt about this.

A person who is bonded by the strings of affection will not have any peace if happiness or sorrows of family life crosses the limits. There is Mirhyu deva waiting for every human being may he be going through childhood, youth or old age.

However there are very few who is aware of the impending fate destined to him. As how a person gets born just like that by himself, same way he passes away leaving all the relations and family with whom he got bonded, the wealth which he had gathered eagerly with great desire, the land which he had acquired with great covetness, leaving all that, as his parents and children are looking with out taking leave or taking leave, without anybody to go along, as he comes alone, he leaves this world alone and passes away.

As soon as a person passes away his body will be laid on the ground like a log of wood and his relations and known people surround him and cry their heart out for his death.

By their cries what will the dead person benefit? If a person had collected wealth by wrong deeds, his wealth will be enjoyed with authority by his people however the sins which accumulate by doing the bad deeds are not shared by the person who enjoy the wealth. The one who has sinned only has to bear the results of his sinful actions while the family may enjoy the wealth without getting affected.

The sinner loaded by the sin will reach hell to undergo the punishments for his sin.

The wealth, which had been collected with sinful means, will stay back at his home. The relations will go to cremation ground with the dead body and after cremating him will get back to their respective homes.

Only the good and bad deeds will go with the soul beyond the cremation ground. The wealth would have been better uoilized by giving it to good poor souls as charity, using it for pilgrimages and going to holy places and by using it to punya obtaining deeds.

The body, which finally becomes the fodder for insects, is a non-permanent thing. The human body will get annihilated either by burning or otherwise. Alas the miser who hoards the wealth is not aware of this simple fact. After he dies the wealth will be definitely carted off by somebody else.

Only a person who has done charity in previous birth becomes a fortunate person in next birth.

However, if a person does charity without any involvement

that charity won't benefit him. Only a person who does charity will get shraddha and bhakti will obtain all the things he wishes for as per his wish.

The great state of Moksha also he can hope to obtain. The Dharma and charity done with bhakti and Shraddha even if it is small like a tiny piece of grain will benefit him like a mountain of deeds.

The great munis who don't have any wealth but reach the blissful abode of the Lord only by their good mind and good deeds.

Hence it is important to keep the mind pure, without that any penance or charities won't fetch any results.

The tool to get Mukti and release from bondage and freedom from the cycle of birth and death is great Bhakti, service to God, charity and dharmic deeds with involvement.

Thus the great truth was taught by Sriman Narayana to the king of birds Garuda.

III

HOW TO GET RID OF THE GHOST FORM AFTER DEATH (PRETHA FORM)

The exalted soul Garuda gave his humble pranams to Sriman Narayana Bhagavan and told `Oh! Vaikunda Varadha, how to get rid of the most bad state a human body can get namely the `pretha janma or ghost form'.

You must kindly tell me this and bless me, prayed the Garuda the king of birds.

Sriman Narayana Bhagawan who is all knowing looked kindly at Garuda and told the following.

Oh! Garuda! I will tell you the karmas, which has to be done when a man dies.

All the persons who want to avoid Pretha Janma should do before one dies, by their own hands Vrishorsartham.

Anyone who dies above five years of age whether he is man or women to avoid pretha janma for him, the person who does karmas for him should do Vrishorsartham.

To avoid ghost form there is no needs to do any other karma apart from this. It can be done when the person is alive or after death. Without doing this vrishorsartham, any other charity or dharma is done or Vratsa's are followed or even yagna's are done that won't take the place of vrishosartham or else the dead person is bound to get the pretha janma.

Hearing this Garuda gave his humble pranams to the Lord and further asked Bhagavan, when this vrishorsargam should be done? If it is done before death which period it has to be done or if it is done after death when is the time it has to be done?. What are the benefits on doing this?

You must kindly tell them tin detail thus prayed the Garuda.

The compassionate God Sriman narayana looked benevolently at Garuda and told ` my child! If the Vrishorsratham is not done for the dead person and in its place other shradhas are done he won't get benefited by that.

For whomever, after the life departs on the 11th day vrishorsargam is not done, than for him pretha janma will definitely happen. This is for sure.

If vrishorsargam is done the dead person instead of obtaining pretha janma,
he will reach the world of ancestors. If he dies in one of the holy places, which helps him in obtaining Jaing Mukthi/liberation, he will not be caught by Lord Yama and will reach a good world.

For whenever vrishorsargam is being done he will also reach such a good world.

This can be done by father, son, wife or grandchild from the daughter or daughter herself can do vrishorsargam to the departed soul. If for the dead person a son is there that son alone should do vrishorsargam, nobody should do it in his place.

Hearing that Garuda the king of birds gave his respects once again to the Lord and enquired further Oh! Sri Vasudeva! If a person dies without any offspring either son or daughter who has to do the kriya karamas for him? Kindly tell clearly about this matter.

For that Sriman Narayanan told ` Dear Kaluza a person without a son will reach only hell and there is no possibility of him reaching a good world.

Hence by doing some sat karma's and tapas a person must try to beget a male child.

If a person does not do any good karmas during his life time and if his children leave out to do the required karmas for the departed person then such a person will roam day and night with great thirst and hunger.

In great agony he will shout `oooo Alas `ooo somebody save me.' Thus shouting for long time he will go round the world, and then get born as insects, mites and such lowly lives.

Then finally get born as human being but in unfortunate wombs only to meet quick deaths again and again. Hence before a person loses his strength to old age and disease and becomes weak to do any karma he must be intelligent to do good karmas to reach the good world.

However if a person instead of doing like that thinks I will do them later and post pones doing the good karmas for the last minute than it is like trying to dig well when the house is on fire.

CHARITY, DHARMIC ACTS AND VRISHORSARGAM

The Garuda who is learned in Vedas worshipped Sriman Narayana who is protector of the entire world and addressing him told ` Hey Paramatma! If a person does charity and good deeds with a pure heart what are the benefits he will get? If his son's and relatives will do charity for him

What are the benefits he will get? If while doing charity it is done in a wrong way what are the effects of that? Kindly tell me these things and bless me.

God Tirumal, lying in his snake bed started telling Garuda the following:

My dear child! Even if charity of 100 cows are done without eagerness to do it and without purity of mind all that won't equal to charity of one cow done with purity of mind as per the rules written in kula.

After a person dies whatever benefit he may get by someone doing for him charity of one-lakh cows will not equal to of he himself doing charity of much fewer cows during his lifetime.

That is why Kaluza, it is better for one person to do charity before his death. The charity should be good. The persons who receive charity also should be good.

The charity should be preferably given in a holy place. The person who gives charity should also be of pure mind. If all these factors join together it will give enormous benefit. The charity given to learned good pandit would increase in benefit day by day. If the person who receives the charity is a good person the person who gives charity will definitely get punya.

The mantras, which are told to bring down the poison, the fire, which has the quality to decrease the cold, does not change in potency by the way it is used.

Same way the person who receives the charity if he is a good person will hold his strength to bless back the person giving charity. Hence while giving charity it should be given to proper person of good mind who is preferably well versed in Vedas and shastras.

If charity is given to a Brahmin who is not having proper discipline and who has no knowledge of Vedas and kula but only holds the name of Brahmin that charity itself will lead the giver to hell.

Further a person who has no qualities to receive charity if he accepts charity he will go to hell taking the taking the next twenty-one generations of his people.

A charity should be given to one person only. If a charity is given to many like a cow given in charity to many will also be the cause to accrue sin.

In case a person who receives the charity sells the article and divides the money with others or if the charity article get passed on from one person to another to be enjoyed by different persons, a person who has given charity will get affected.

He will stay in hell for a long time. However a person who gives charity of good things to deserving good persons will get the good results of charity definitely in this birth or next birth without fail.

He can as well consider the benefits of charity as a concrete thing, which is put in a box and is in safekeeping. If a rich person dies in case his children do charity and karmas with great shradhha and pure mind, whatever good he will augur will soill be less compared to even a very poor person who does not have issues but if he does charity as per his affordability during his living time by his own hand.

My dear child! How a person traveling to neighbouring city if he carries his food can travel without worrying about hunger. In the same way each person when he is alive itself does charity of food and other things, after death he can travel freely without hunger and thirst and reach a good world comfortably.

As how a person traveling without proper provision will suffer on the way, same way a person who does not do any charity in his life time will suffer great agonies on way after death.

The good karmas and charity done in a holy place at a holy time will grow like a fire fed by ghee (clarified butter).

However even if a charity is done in a not so holy place and not a holy time but along with charity if the karma of vrishorsargam is done and even if charity done to a not so deserving Brahmin due to the punya karma of Vrishorsargam's greatness whatever benefit one may get by giving charity to a deserving Brahmin in a correct time in a holy place will be obtained.

Thus for a person to reach a good state the karma which helps him vrishorsargam.

My dear Garuda it is not proper to assume the one who is present today will be there tomorrow also. The human body is impermanent.

Instead of thinking good deeds and good acts can be done tomorrow, the good karmas should be done as and when one thinks.

Even a person blessed with a son, if he does not do any charity or dharma acts by his own hands and passes away, he will not reach a good state.

However a person having no children if he does good deed

and die, he will reach a good state.

More than doing yagna and giving charity like cow, the best thing to do is vrishorsargam. It is the best and exalted karma.

IV
The vrishorsargam karma

Either in full moon at karthika month or in any other good day, or uthrayana time at sukla paksha or even at Krishna paksha or during ekadasi with a pure heart in a exalted holy place on a good tidhi day, on a good yoga nakshtra time, in a good manner, inviting Brahmins who are learned in Vedas and Kula after invoking Gods, making oneself pure, after doing puja of Navagraha and doing archana of mother devata, offering puranahadhi doing shardha in name of maha Vishnu, a rishiba calf has to be bathed with water sanctified by mantras.

Then decorating it with cloth, ornaments and sweet smelling flowers, further joining it with four more male calves make the rishbha calf to go around the fire, then facing the north direction looking at the rishbha calf one has to tell `

Oh! Dharma, you only become rishiba, you only was created first by Brahman thus telling if the calf is given in charity in name of dead person or if the person does it for himself, thinking for oneself the water sanctified by mantras is poured on the tail and the water is to be collected in the hand and sprinkled on the head and the rishiba calf should be left free along with other male calves.

Garuda! If the vrishorsargam is done for the dead person then immediately ekadihsta shradh has to be done. In case the person is doing for himself then he must give something, which he is very fond of as charity to Brahmins.

Without doing vrishorsargam it is not possible to avoid pretha (ghost) form. Hence without doing vrishorsargam to one's benefit if one does lot of good karmas and after death the son's and others do many good karmas for the departed soul, it won't be much use to avoid the pretha janma.

THE WAY TO GO TO YAMA LOKA

The student of Veda vyasa muni Sriman Suutha Puraniga addresses the Namacharanya residents, the Maharishis there and told those great munis of high penance-

The conversation between the king of the birds Garuda and Lord Narayana- Garuda gave his humble pranams to Lord Narayana and addressing him as the Lord of the whole world, asked him, `how far is Yamaloka form here? What is its character? You should kindly tell about these things and bless us.'

Hearing these queries the compassionate one, the dark colored Lord started telling as such

Dear Garuda! The distance between the world where human being live and the Yamapuri, there is 860000, kada distance. In that Yamaloka lives Yamadharma Raja.

He sends his messengers to the world when the Life period ends of a Jive to bring him to Yama puri. His messengers are of different types.

Some have forms, which scares anyone who gets to see them. Some have red shot eyes and fierce angry look. They have weapons like noose and musalam, their clothes are jet black like the rain cloud.

When the life period ends of a jive they tie by noose and with the body form of the jive converted to one like air, they lock the same in a container and take him to Yamaloka.

After reaching there these Jives who have form like ghost will be presented to the head of Yamapuri the Kala deva, the Yama raja stating to him `Oh! Yama raja, as per your order the jive who has completed his lifetime is brought and presented in front of you, now as per your order we are ready to follow further action, thus telling they stand on a side.

The Yamadharma Raja who is the rider of `Mahesh or Buffalo will address thus his messengers.

`Hey Kinkara, Good, take the Jive again back and leave him in the house where he has died and bring him back on 12th day from today and present him again thus he will order."

Immediately these Yamaduthas in a second tying the jive, crossing the

86,000 kada length once more will reach the jive back to its house.

Thus the jive since he goes to Yamalok and returns back again to Bhulok to its place, the dead person's body should not be immediately burnt or cremated. Only after a while such an act should be done.

The jive who had been tied by the Yamaduth in his spirit form by the string of pasha, as soon as it gets untied, the spirit form of that jive goes to the cremation ground and observes its body from above looking it being burnt.

It finds there is no way for it to enter it again. It laments seeing his body thus getting destroyed, crying Oh! Alas! How sad!. However if the jive is a punya atma, it will feel happy that whatever happens is for the good.

`Let the body be burnt' Oill the body which is in the pyre gets completely burnt and turned to ash, especially oill the head gets burned completely the jive will not loose its attachment to its body, the things connected with the body, its relations and other things connected with the life in that body.

In the burning pyre as soon as the body from the head to foot get completely burned, the jive will start acquiring the pinda form of body.

It forms in a gradual process. From the pindam offered by the son of the dead person on the first day the head gets formed. From the pindam offered on the second day the neck and shoulder gets formed. The third day pindam helps in forming chest, fourth day pindam forms stomach, fifth day forms the buttocks, sixth day forms `prishtam. 'Seventh day forms `kayyam.' The 8th day pindam forms thighs, ninth day pindam forms legs and the tenth day pindam forms the full body.

On formation of the Pinda body, the jive arrives to the house where it was living previously with its family. There without entering the house, it observes the persons who enter and leave the house and with great agony suffering from pangs of hunger and thirst it will cry piteously.

That jive in the pinda form partakes whatever its son offers through the route of the Brahman,. On the 13th day the as per the order of Yamadharama, the yamaduths arrives there and ties the jive in pinda form with the chord of pasha (attachment) and drags him away. The jive in great attachment keeps looking at his house again and again repeatedly and crying piteously reaches the Yamalok.

Garuda! The jive in his pinda form tied by the chord of pasha, dragged by yamaduths has to walk per day 247 kada distance day and night. Along the way he has to pass through wooded forest having sharp thorny plants.

At the same time the jive has to suffer pangs of hunger and thirst. It is indeed difficult to describe the misery the jive undergoes enroute. Let it be so.

Further along the jive's route there is a town called Vaivatham. This town has many high raised buildings. It is the dwelling place of other jives looking scary and grotesque. It gives great pain to see such creatures. Many papa jives who stay there can be heard crying piteously Ah! Ah! Oo.

Only boiling hot water can be had there for drinking. Not a drop of water fit for drinking will be available there. The clouds there rain blood instead of water from above. Didn't I state the jive who died will be taken to Yamapuri on 13th day? Listen to its state.

Like dragging a monkey and taking it along the Yamaduthas on the 10th day tie the jive, which is now in pinda form with the chord made of pasha (attachment), that jive will be lamenting thinking about his son and other close relations.

Oh! Alas my dear son! Here I am undergoing untold sufferings! Ooooo...... What can I do? What can I do? There is someone called God Almighty and heaven, to reach there good and bad conducts are the yardstick, such information and thoughts were not conceded by me when I stayed in the mortal world with my body and life.

Oh! Alas when I was told about the cause of life and death and states beyond death, I sniggered and laughed at such persons. Where is God? Whatever is told about papa and punya are only flights of imagination, thus I jeered at the good souls, wise ones and renounced sanyasis who tried to preach about this.

I laughed at their words and made fun at them. Alas! I am experiencing the fruits of my actions now. I find I am unable and helpless to do anything by my strength or effort now. All alone now I am suffering helplessly. The Yamaduths with their formidable weapons without an iota of compassion are punishing me now. Ooo...... oo...

Why I did not do any good deeds when I lived in the mortal world. Indeed, I did not help the elderly and infirm persons; I did not go for any pilgrimage. I did not preach or listen to any words of wisdom.

Nor did I support and follow the yogis and munis who were trying to preach to people words of wisdom.

Indeed I had not felt for other jives as my brethren, I did not even arrange drinking water spots in places where people did not have water to drink.

I did not do any of the welfare work like digging a well; make green pastures for the cows to graze. In fact I claimed the general land as my own land. Now without any land, property without a body also I am roaming as a ghost form and suffering with great agonies.

If only I had done charity when I lived in the earth!! Rather I looked down on Vedas and Shastras. I laughed at the puranic stories as just a pack of fictional tale.

I did not make any provision to make schools for the children wanting to get educated, nor did I buy and donate good moral books like Ramayana and Mahabharata.

Nor did I pay heed to words of elders, least I could have invited the pandits to talk about puranic stories and looked up to the same, but alas! I did not do it.

On the punya day of Sri Hari, the ekadasi day I did not do any fasting. Oh! How sad I did not even dream to do any good deed which would have got for me punya.

With complete ignorance of the world beyond I was only happy doing actions which augured for me sin. Now to whom will I tell and cry, repent about the actions and life, which I had lived wrongly.

Thus crying piteously the papa jive beaten and dragged by the yamaduthas is being taken to Yamapuri.

Thus told Suutha puranigar to Garuda as being the words told by the greatNarayana Himself.

V

THE PAPA JIVES SUFFERINGS REROUTE

Suutha Puranigar addressed the Naimacahranya residents as `Ardent bhaktis of Lord Narayana' and told here is the extract of Lord Narayan's preaching to Lord Garuda.

`The Jive who is tied by the Yamaduthas with the chord of pasha (attachment) and who gets beaten, dragged and taken away thinks about the happy time he had in the mortal world with his family and children, but lo! Now in a dire state with pangs of hunger and thirst, tired and fatigued laments in a despairing voice.

O... Where are my family and children who stayed with me? Where are my parents, relations and others? Oh! Where are my dear friends? Where are my servants who obey to my bidding? Alas everyone has left me alone like this to be tortured by these yamaduthas.

Indeed I recall the amount of wealth I collected at times by deceit and resorting to falsehood, using my brain to cleverly manipulate situations in my favour.

However where is now all the wealth and comfort collected. With my power I enjoyed many times public wealth for personal gain, I had drawn the work of poor workers to feed my family and relations.

I was keen that my family should enjoy all the comforts for which I had not hesitated to take away others due, even against the call of my conscience.

However are any my family members and relations who had enjoyed the benefits of my wealth and deeds are here now? Is any single one of them here to bear these miseries?

Oh! Alas why did I do such deceitful and bad deed for my folks and who are now enjoying the wealth while I am dragged and made to answer for my misdeeds.

Thinking back, at that time persons who implicitly believed I am a good person and lost their hard earned wealth to my ministrations. But on knowing about the loss of their wealth how much heart burn they would have felt. Now I am undergoing many fold more sufferings for my deeds O... O.. what can I do now? What to do? Thus the jive cried in agony.

Hearing the Jive crying and wailing the Yamaduthas who drag and take him get exasperated. They give the jive some sharp blows in his cheek and tell! Hey fool! You got some sense now only?

When you were in the mortal world you thought, you alone have the worthy family, kith and kin. Your life alone is important and worthy to take care of. Further you assumed your family is permanent. Thus living in the false world you did not bother to do any dharma deed.

You freely followed the path of adharma to live the life of luxury. But where are your own people to help you now at the time of distress? The good and bad deed you did alone is capable of giving you happiness and sorrow here.

When you lived in the earth, in the mortal world you spend your time and energy for pleasures of the body. On things, which gave excitement and pleasure to your body and mind were the ones you went for.

You freely gave the wealth to the ones who gave you these pleasures but when the hard working persons asked their due, even when they pleaded with you in great distress, you behaved haughoily and with some clever ways of talking turned them away, while you had no qualms to squander and give away your wealth to the ones like prostitutes to enjoy the pleasures of the body.

Your humanitarian feeling is only to be shown to young girls isn't it?
Do those persons who received your wealth so generously are here to help you at the time of reckoning?

Are they here to put a balm on your writhing wound? If only you had acted in dharmic and truthful ways why you have to come to state like this? Why should you get caught in our hands and become helpless now?

Why should you be lamenting and crying now in agony? Why are you staring at us as though we are the one's making you suffer.

Thus admonishing the jive again giving a sound thrashing to it by the chord of pasha and cane they were holding, the Yamaduths drags the jive and prods him to move ahead.

Garuda! Look at the state of person's doing misdeeds.

`Then that `chetna' further travels along the road of wind and for a while along the dense forest filled with wild animals like huge tigers. Here the exhausted jive is allowed to rest for a while.

On 28th day of his death the jive partakes the pindam offered by his son after a shradha. Then on 30th day he reaches a place called `Yamiyam' where preta atma's would be seen in large numbers.

There will be also river called `Punya pathra' and number Banyan trees. The jive stays here for a while, taking a bit rest but with constant fear of the yamakingras. Here it partakes the second masika pindam.

Then it further gets dragged by yamakingras and goes through another dense fearful forest. All along the route it cries with great agony O...O.. not able to bear the torture meted out by the yamakingras time to time.

Then it reaches a city called `souri' belonging to the king called `Sangaman. Here it partakes the 3rd month's masika pindam.

As it comes out of this city it has to pass through a region of unbearable cold. As it cringes in the cold the yamakingras join together and pelt it with stones in anger.

After these difficulties it reaches a city called `Kura puram' where it partakes the fifth masika pindam. Then walking further it reaches a place called Krilancham and here it partakes sixth month masika pindam.

It stays here for half a Muhurtha time. Then starts from there now going along a fearful route. As it goes along again it remembers about the good life on earth and its family and friends thinking about the present state it cries piteously.

Hearing its cries the yamakingras in great anger thrash him and ask him to close his mouth.

As the jive moves further in great pain, it meets large groups of boatmen who have large fearful form and they approach with burning torches
they confront the jive `Hey jive! Have you ever done a charity called `Vaitharni godahnam', in which you give in charity of a cow in name of this fearful river in front of you?

If you have done that we will help you to cross the river peacefully. If not we have to push you inside this river and submerge you deep oill your reach pathal.

Hey Jive! This vaitharni river is 100 yojana long. Don't think being a river it is filled with water. In place of water this river is filled with blood and pus, urine and excreta. It is the dwelling place of fearful creatures. It is filled with such putrefying smell that even creatures without a nose to sense the smell cannot bear it.

Oh! jive if you have done charity of even a single cow at the time of living in the mortal world, that punya will help you to cross the river and go to the other bank without problem. However if you have not done any such charity you have to fall into this river and for a long time stay there and cross it by yourself.

Oh! Lord of the sky, Garuda! Since every jive who lives and dies has to cross this Vaitharani river on its way to Yamalok, it is told in the scriptures that every jive, at least the ones born in Bharata desha has to do the charity called Vaitharani Godhan, where charity of a cow is given to the deserving person.

In case the jive does not do it at the time he is alive in the mortal world, after he dies his son can do godhan in his name. If such a charity has been done than the jive crosses the Vaitharani river easily and goes to the country at Vichithiran and there it partakes the seventh masika pindam.

To those jives who have not done such charity when they are about to partake the seventh masika pindam, lot of pretha atmas with grotesque form come in front of him and tell ` Hey- fool, when you lived in the mortal world, you thought of yourself as a big man and you treated with contempt persons who came and pleaded from you some charity.

You not only did not give them any but also made fun of them. Is it not? Now for your hunger the pindam which is sent to you and which you are eagerly trying to partake, this food does not belong to you, give that to us, and so saying they snatch it from him and take it away.

Oh! King of birds! Even if you have lived in the mortal world without any wealth as a pauper, soill to persons who had come seeking your charity, if you had not denied them but given whatever possible by you than you are saved.

A jive who had refused to help his brethren and also ridiculed them will on death be dragged and brought to this country called `Vichithram' by yamaduthas and definitely the pindam offered to him by his son will not reach him but the ghosts will snatch it form him and only scattered few bits of food he has to collect and eat lamenting,

Oo... alas! when I was down in the world I not only ate and grew fat but also hid and stored the food away from others eyes and even refused to give to anyone who pleaded and asked for food.

Is it all the sin, which I had thus accumulated that this route to yamalok is turning out to be most difficult journey! That I am terribly suffering with hunger and thirst, my lips are getting parched and tongue withdrawn, I am besieged with untold miseries and there is no one with whom I can share my agonies except the yamakingras and ghosts.

I am getting back in equal measure for the sin of denial I did for the persons who had come in front of me tired and famished seeking some food, when I was alive in the world below I did not bother to give them even a morsel of food.

Did I at least believe the mahans who indicated the state after death? Alas no, I was nonchalant, I thought whatever may happen after death, now that I am alive and well why to worry. Now whom to tell the troubles I am undergoing here? Thus the jive laments.

That time the Yamakingras who are near him tell ` Oh! You are complete fool. You had the rare opportunity to be born in the earth as a human being. That sort of birth is the best one a jive can aspire for which is capable of giving him everything and whatever he wants like a boon giving `karpaka tree' What can be better birth than that of a human being?

He could have done plenty of dharma, charity, puja for the present and future and collected lots and lots of punya. Instead of that the human being who spends his time in collecting things that are of no use to future state, what to tell of him?

In the human form while living in the mortal world, whatever good and bad deed one does, the fruits of these acts alone the person experiences after his death in the other worlds.

After death when the jive moves in ghost /pretha form in other worlds he is unable to do punya or papa acts.

A jive reaches an exalted world and enjoys or reaches a lowly world and suffers as a result of his acts in human form.

A human being getting the comfort and luxuries in human form ,a jive taking the form of a master and another the servant are all the fruits of papa and punya acts done by him. However what is the use of knowing these in this state?

Garuda! There is a charity called `Uthaha Kumba dhanam'. If such a charity is done for the jive by his son or others for the jive, the jive will be able to drink little bit of water from the kumba to quench his thirst and on seventh month it will start moving from there.

Oh! King of birds! As the jive has now crossed half way to its destination to Yamapuri, that month his people in the mortal world should give food to deserving persons (Brahmins).

Further that jive will move to the country called `pakuva padam' and there it partakes $8^{th}$ month pindam offered to it by its son. Starting from there it will then reach a place called `Dukadam'.

There it will undergo deep sorrow reflecting its state. There it partakes 9th masika pindam. Moving from there it reach a place called `nathakrantham' staying there it partakes tenth masika pindam.

In that place lot of jives in groups can be seen roaming about in pretha form, as `Vrisharahanam' is not done by them or for them hence the jives have taken to pretha form. They can be seen crying out moving in great agony shouting.

O Alas! when this state will end. Seeing such fellow jives in pretha form this jive would get greatly disturbed and will cry its heart out seeing all the sorrow going on.

Then moving further it will reach a country called `athaptham' 'and partakes the $11^{th}$ masika pindam. Then after staying there for a while moves to a place called `Sitapuram'. There it will get vexed by chill and cold and here it partakes 12th masika pindam.

Starting from there it looks pathetically at all the four directions and at the yamakingras who are dragging and taking him and cries in a helpless manner` Yamakingras!

Where is my partner who promised to stay with me forever? Where is my lover who vouched not to get attached to anyone except me? Where is my dearest friend who promised to be with me in thick and thin? Where are my children and rest of the family? What will this poor soul do now?

Hearing its wail yamadhutas look with contempt at the jive and say` what a complete fool are you? Do you expect to see your partner and family and people even now?

Have you not left your attachment to them even now? Here you can see only the fruits of your papa and punya, thus talking they thrash the jive to submission.

Hearing the statement of yamakingras the jive further wails Oh! O I forgot what you told me already about my family and people.

I am only incoherently rumbling thus it tries to stop its lamentation and bottles up its feelings with in itself and moves on. Before reaching the Vivastha patnam it partakes the unapathika pindam and then reaches the patanam.

That Vaivastha patanam (city) is the Yamapuri. That Yamapuri is 144 kada in length. It is populated by Gandharva, apsaras and others, totally populated by 84,000 jives. The 12 sravanas also reside in that country who understanding the papa and punya the jives do and report the same to Yamadharma Raja.

The jives who land there have to worship and to aradhana
of the sravanas

VI

THE TWELVE SRAVANAS WHO ANALYZE AND TELL THE JIVES THE FRUITS OF THEIR PAPA AND PUNYA ACTS.

Sutha muni addressed the Sounakathi munis and told a follows.

`Hey respectful munis here I will tell you what preaching transpired between Garuda and Lord Narayana.

Lord Garuda fell on the feet of Sriman Narayana who is personification of compassion and entreated Him `Oh! Lord Perumal, the compassionate one tell me, who are that 12 sravanas? Whose children they are? What is the reason of their stay at Vaivastha patnam? How the Sravanas come to know the papa and punya deeds done by human beings? Please tell about all these.

Hearing Garudas's plea, Lord Narayana happily started preaching him thus-
`Oh! King of birds! Listen to me, At one time Lord Maha Vishnu, the lord of the entire universe was alone, holding the entire universe and all the jives with in Him.

That time from the navel of Maha Vishnu appeared a long stemmed lotus. From the lotus came out the four faced god Lord Brahma.

Lord Brahma then did a long and arduous penance on Sri Hari Narayana and learned about all the Vedas and methods of creation. Then he did the act of creation itself and created this universe and everything here.

As soon as creation occurred the devas as Urithiran and other devas started doing their respective works. Among the devas one of the real talented deva the Yamadharma reached the country called `Gemini' and started ruling it.

He was interested on knowing correctly the punya and papa acts done by the jives. He started trying to know the same. But however much he tried he could not clearly know their acts.

Hence Yamadharma felt unhappy and went to the four faced Brahma and after giving Him his pranams told `Oh! Lord Brahma, I tried very hard to know the papa and punya acts of jives with a wish to punish and protect them.

I stayed in Gemini nagar for long and tried to understand it. But I am soill unable to clearly know the acts of jives done at the mortal world. Only if I know that I will be able to punish the papis and protect the punya atmas. Hence kindly bless me to realize these and give me the power to do the needful for the same.

Hearing this request, Lord Brahma took a stalk of darpa grass and threw it down with a boon, `Let the one's with long eyes and endowed with beautiful perfect bodies the `sravanas ' who will keep a watch and listen to the papa and punya acts of the jives and will be your messenger informing and helping you to decide the course of action'

Thus the twelve shravanas came about helping Yamadharma raja in doing right dharma to the residents of the mortal world and to carry them properly along the path of birth and death.

Garuda! For the papa atmas this Dharmapuri will look fearful. Dharmaraja and his duthas will appear in fearful form creating terror and scarce in the mind and that papa atma will cry out fearfully looking at them.

However for the one who has done punya, the Yamadharma raja will appear like a compassionate king. He will be highly pleased seeing the Yamadharma and will wonder at the greatness of god seeing the yamapuri.

Though Yamadhara raja is one, he will appear fearful to papi and divine to punya atmas. When punya atma goes near Lord Yama, the yamadharma raja will immediately stand up from his seat giving respect to punya atma and bless him. ` Let this punya atma go along the surya marg to Brahmalok'

However the papi jive will further suffer if for the dead jive in the mortal world proper `masika sodha kumbha' are not done. That jive will be not only tied by chord of pasha, but will be beaten and thrashed, dragged like cattle.

Later seeing to the papa, punya the jive will be ordained next form of life. However before that as per the orders of Yamadharma, the papa jive will be sent to hell. If his papa's are more he may get janma of insects and other crawling animals.

But if his punya is on higher side he will get a human form like before. If he had done lot of dharma and charity then without fail he will receive the fruits of his charity in the next birth.

A man when he is alive in this world may think` I am an important person, I am blessed with wealth and strength. I am a very intelligent person. He may get name and fame as a great scientist, leader of a religious group, as a great king and so on.

However as soon as he dies his body will be stripped of everything and preparation will be made for destruction of the body either by putting him in a grave and burying him or burning him in a pyre, at times thrown to vultures and animals as food.

However it is rare and fortunate for a jive to get human form. Even if he gets a human form to get a whole complete form without any of his sense impaired is a fortunate thing.

Soill more fortunate is to be born in a good family having good moral values.

When a jive is so born if it does not strive for the objective of birth namely to attain mukti or liberation from cycle of birth and death then it will be like getting a pot full of precious nectar and instead of having the nectar if a person puts the pot down and spills away the nectar wastefully, it will amount to the that, if a person wastes his life on useless matters

VII
THE TROUBLES, THE PRETA JANMA CREATES.

Garuda gave his pranams to lord Kesava and told 'Swami among sin which sin which make jive get the preta janma? Does he move in the preta form in the mortal world or else will he be under the command of lord Yama in and around Yamapuri'? All these kindly tell me in details.

'Oh! Lord of the skies! Whoever snatches others wealth and wife, he alone after death gets the Vayu like form of preta janma, and it will be vexed with hunger and trust it will be roaming ever where even coming out of Yama's cordon.

When a person is dead and his body is lying in his house, when another person who is not bit grieving about the death but with his intelligence manages to cart away the wealth and properties of the dead person, that person will become a preta Janma and roam around in all the hell.

He will further disturb and create harm to his own family members and relations. Since he will be preta form on the day of the pituru (ancestors) he won't allow the pituru to get inside the house but will drive them away.

He will snatch the food offered to pituru and will partake the same. That preta atma will see that the wealth in the house will not be enjoyed the family members, nor given in charity to others but get simply wasted.

He will see that his son and others in the family don't get any progeny and his race does not proceed further. He will send diseases and different fevers to the family members and make them suffer.

Than the king of birds Garuda further asked Lord Vishnu the Adi Murthy 'what more the preta atma will do? How will he look like? How to know a person has obtained preta Janma in one family?' Kindly tell me all these and bless me.

Sriman Narayana tells, Vanideya! The one who has acquired Preta Janma will trouble one's own family, kith and kin but for the one who does dharmic acts, charities, sing kirtan's of lord Hari, do shradhas regularly for ancestors and go for pilgrimage the Preta Janma cannot do any harm.

Ones who do not do dharmic and charitable acts, who ridicule bhakti's one's how has no faith in god, who consume flesh of animals and liquor, who habitually tell lies are the ones who get troubled by Preta Janma.

Their troubles will increase, like they will get induced to do more and more sinful acts, they won't get any male children and continuously get only girl child, they will fall out will their own people, quarrelling with them, they don't get opportunity to take care of cows.

They will get repeatedly a lot of troubles and miseries in life; they will loose their friends in misunderstanding, and on the upashana day of ekadashi they may end up eating wrong foods.

They will waste their life without seeking god Hari and they may not get opportunity to japa and Homas to improve the Karma in life. They will fall in love below their station.

They will ill-treat their own mother and father; they even turn to murder and other heinous crimes. They won't benefit from fruits of a good harvest. They will earn their lively hood not by honourable work but only by demeaning works.

Always there inclination will be to do adharma and they may lack courage. Their wealth may get destroyed by fire and litigation. Their health will be constantly affected with problems like severe stomach-ache, headache, etc.

They will look down upon puranas and scriptures srutis and smritis. They will have no respects for elders and bakthi for god. If at all they want to do any rites for ancestors, it will get obstructed.

The good looks from their face may get blemished. Their son will become like enemy and bad mouth him. He may have to undergo long separation from his wife and end up quarrelling with her for some reason or other.

All this trouble is created by the Preta Janma who had been born in his own family and dead now. Garuda! In which over family will Preta Janma dosha(curse) is there that family will be sounded by sorrows and troubles.

The Preta Janma with fearful face and sharp pointed teeth will appear in the dream of family members and cry out 'Ow' is not their anyone in this family to save me. I am suffering from great hunger and thirst when my Preta form will leave me'.

COMPENSATION DONE HER DOSA (Fault) & DOING PUJA TO THE PRIME PERSONS.

Residents of Naimacharanya! As Garuda heard about the pretha janma and its actions, he worshipped Lord Narayanamurthy and asked tell me Janarthana! The one who has obtained pretha janma, when he will come out of it? For how much time a person will be held in pretha janma? Kindly tell me about these too" thus he prayed.For that Tirumal started replying thus,

Oh! King of birds! The ones who have obtained pretha janma may come in the dream of his family person or at times may not come in his dream but will bring about his ill acts in a `gupt' manner.

Whether the pretha janma reveals itself or not when the family members get besieged and troubled by the pretha janma, then immediately they should consult learned elders and follows the dharmic path and does the good deeds prescribed by them.

This may be like, to plant useful trees as mango, coconut tree, flowering plants like jasmine, champak and shade giving pepal trees. They can also form a nice garden and plant in it good flowering plants in them. To good deserving persons they can give farming lands as charity. For the cow and cattle to graze they can maintain good grazing lands. They can dig ponds for water.

They can do work connected with temple activities like arranging and participating in satsangs. They can take bath in punya holy rivers like Ganga, Yamuna, Kaveri, and Thamrabarani and do dharma and charity. Whenever they are besieged by troubles and sorrow those times they have necessarily have to do these acts with keenness and faith.

If it is not done this way the troubles will increase more and more. Even as a result of blocks created by prethajanma they may not get inclined to do dharmic deeds.

Even the buddhi does not get inclined and they may not get any bhakti to do these acts, whoever does with spirit these dharmic deeds he will reap the fruits. Because of his dharmic deeds the one who has attained pretha janma also becomes happy and will reach the world of ancestors and there he will shed his pretha body.It will then help in begetting a child who will propagate his vamsa or lineage.

Lord Garuda then raises a doubt to Lord Narayana who is expounding the merits and demerits of the different actions performed.

Oh! Lord ` say if one is not aware a person in one's family has obtained pretha janma, nor the pretha janma comes into the dream and tell him of its existence, that being so in case he gets lot of repeated troubles and say he approaches elders and learned ones and asks why he is besieged with troubles, in turn the learned one's inform him it must be due to dosha's of pretha janma, that time what all things he has to do? Kindly tell me about them.

To his query Lord Narayana started telling thus-

Oh! King of birds! At those times one must certainly believe in what the learned ones tell. By doing actions which will lead to purification like bath, japa, homa, charity, penance one has to clear one's papas. Further one has to do Narayana Bali.

However without clearing one's papa's if one tries to do Naryana bali, then it may encounter further hindrance from other buta and pretha forms. Hence it is very important to clear one's sins or do compensating acts and then do rituals and other sacrifices.

During punya days who ever does charity in pilgrimage places in the name of ancestors, he will never be disturbed by buta, pretha and pichachu forms.

For a man his father, mother and Guru are the three known gods. They get the place of worship as they help in forming their body and as they teach good morals while bringing one up Hence at any time it is important for one to worship them.

They must follow their instructions and lead life. A person who worships one's parents even if he abstains from worship of gods soill he will be excused.

However if a person is not devoted to his parents he does not obey their commands and even if he does all the sacred acts like respecting a Brahmin, going to renowned places of worship all that will not fetch him any merits.

However after the parents die who ever does dhana(charity) and dharma deeds in their name he will reap the fruits without fail.

Since a son helps to cross one's parents from a hell called `puth' a son is being called `puthar'. Whoever does not follow the words of one's father, mother but heed the words of one's spouse and others will fall lower and lower in his karmic acts.

Oh! Garuda no death rites should be done to person who dies falling into water bodies like river, well, sea etc. Also for those who are put to death by sword or gun and those who commit suicide.

One should wait for a year after their death and then do the rites.

Before doing the rites no auspicious acts like marriage, special charities should be done. One should not undertake acts like pilgrimage and other religious acts. At the end of the year the rites should be done for the departed, and then every auspicious act can be done.

VIII
THE REASONS FOR OBTAINING PRETHA JANMA

As Sriman Narayana gave these explanations Garuda Bhagawan bends and gave his oblations to Lord and enquired Oh! Auspicious Lord, Treasure of all virtues! Due to what sins one jive obtains Pretha Janma? Will he eat? Where will he stay? Kindly illuminate me with these knowledge".

Hearing these Lord Narayana looked at the king of birds and told the following

Oh! Garuda who ever does great sins in the mortal world will obtain pretha janma. If one has done noble deeds like digging wells, pond and lakes, if he has done charity acts like erecting free water and food distributing centers, if he had made rest houses, temples which are coming to use for many people then goodness will be recorded against his being.

However his progeny or his descendant, who gets hold of his possession after death and if he misses his charity, sell the same to make money, such a person will get pretha janma.

A person who robs the land belonging to another person and a person who occupies the land belonging to the border of his village, takes up that property as his own, also the land belonging to common use like gardens or forest land as his own or if a person reclaims the common use land of ponds wells etc. and adds it to his property.

Also persons who meets his death killed by a `chandala' (Persons performing lowly duties) or if a person gets killed by wild animals also the one who meets his death by natural calamities like thunder bolt, by falling into the fire or takes his life by burning himself, one who dies hit by a bull, one who takes life by hanging himself, by taking poison or get killed by weapons or the one who dies without having anyone to do his rites, one who dies without any one aware of his death in far off places, the one who dies killed by robbers, the one who dies without doing Vrishorshradam to the one who does not do shradh or death rites to one's own parents will attain pretha janma.

Oh! Vinadeya! If a Brahmin dies all the rites connected with his death should be done by a Brahmin only. The one who dies, whichever caste he belongs to that caste person alone should do the rites to the person.

Without following these dictums if things for doing rites like cow dung dried, hay, rice etc. are carried by a non-Brahmin to the cremation ground then the dead Brahmin and the person who carries the things to the cremation ground both will obtain pretha janma.

A person who falls from the mountain or mountain slope and dies, a person who dies while sleeping in the cot or while lying in the cot awake, a person who dies in places above the ground (staying in higher stories), a person who dies without uttering the names of the lord or dies after coming in contact with brothel women or touching chandala and without taking bath and purifying himself. A person who dies in house where women with periods are staying will obtain pretha janma.

Also persons who lay un verified blame on one's own mother, wife, daughter, daughter in laws regarding their bad conduct and condemns them will obtain pretha janma.

Persons who subscribe justice against what is written in Manu smriti, persons who are party in killing or torturing cows and good Brahmins, persons who partake alcohol and other intoxicating products, persons who has relation with guru's wife, persons who rob white silk, gold etc will get the pretha janma.

The persons who get pretha janma will always be roaming in dry deserts struggling for bare subsistence.

RULES FOR BIRTH AND DEATH

Garuda Bhagavan gave his oblations to Adi Bhagawan and started his questions. Oh! Sarvesa! Is it not in this mortal world, there are four varnas of people namely Brahmins, kshatriyas, Vaisyas and shudras.

In them whoever the jive is whether he is young, a small child, old person, rich, poor, a compassionate person, a philanthropist, a miser, or he is wise, ignorant, erudite, a pandit, or illiterate, whether he is a king or a pauper, he is a exalted Brahmin, or belonging to a very low caste all of them stay in this mortal world for a prescribed time and then pass away.

What is the reason for their limited stay in this mortal world and then passing away, you must kindly tell the reason or mystery behind their birth and death.

The lord whose existence is in this and beyond this world, Lord Nedumal looked at Garuda and told Oh! Vainadeya! Your question is a very good one, I am giving you the answer for it hear `When it is time for living jive to die, a form called `kalan' comes to fore. It is the `kalan' who takes the jive's life from its body by various means.

The jives that live in this world get their life span decreased due to various papa's / doshas they accumulate due to their wrong deeds. Some of the doshas are as here I am explaining- the one who has desire for another person's wife have their life span decreased.

The one who has failed to do good deeds which stand as foundation to life in this world and the world above, the one who has failed to respect elders and follow their dictates and one who is not pure at heart, one who has no reverence to God, one who knowingly does sins will be going to hell from Yamaloka and stay there for long.

The one who thinks bad for others, the one who does bad for others, one who tells lies, the one who has no compassion for other jives, the one who does not live as prescribed in the sastrtas, the one who tries to do the duties assigned to others and not focus on his own duties will undergo miseries in Yamalok.

The days one does not do japa and prayers, the days one does not worship the great mahans who have done good to humanity, and think about persons who have done good acts for the welfare of others, the days one does not go to temple and holy shrines, the days one does not contemplate about the scriptures those days are wasted in one's life.

However the one born in sudhra or untouchable community should assume the one born in Brahmin (higher) community as living Gods and do the jobs assigned to him by them dutifully then he will reach a good state by those acts itself.

It is not necessary for him to do any other special karma for redemption. If he does service for the one higher force he will reach his elevation.

Garuda! What to talk of human body alone, any jive born in this mortal world is impermanent and without strong foundation. It is just formed by the food partaken.

The food eaten in the morning for a full stomach gets digested and get over by evening. Again hunger gnaws the vitals. If food is not eaten again the body will become weak and start falling apart. Thus the body is highly impermanent.

It is formed as a result of the karmic deeds. Hence one should try not to get trapped again and again in this impermanent and fast disintegrating body. Thus not to again come back to this mortal world one should try to do good deeds.

Oh! Vinadeya! Is it possible to tell whom this body belongs to, to the one, which is coming out of the previous deeds? Does it belong to the jive which unnecessarily carries it and get troubled? Can it be told it belongs to the guardian who provides it food and cloth? Does it belong to the father who is the cause of pregnancy and its birth? Or does it belong to mother who carries it for 10 months and gives birth to it? Does it belong to grandmother who gave birth to mother of the jive?

Does it belong to grandfather who was instrumental in bringing out the father of the jive? Does it belong to master who owns the jives and make him work and pay for him? Does it belong to the employer? Does it belong to the fire that consumes the jive and converts it to ash? Does it belong to wild animals like wolves that devour the body of the jive after he passes away/ or to the insects and worms that feed on the body left after the life has gone? Alas it does not belong to any one of them.

Knowing this truth one should not unduly get attached to this body but should put the mind in Bhagavat, Bhagavan and other holy acts. Sins are committed by mind, word and action. The one who sins more gets birth as dog, wolf and other low lives.

When the jive comes to the womb his trouble starts. Initially he gets troubled by the urine and fetus of the mother. The birth also is a traumatic and painful one.

Knowing the troubles one has to undergo in birth itself as well as death, the jive should live abiding in good conducts and try to avoid the next births.

The one who is born out of mother's womb remains ignorant in childhood life in youth is involved in the passions of youth and growing up. Thus at those times he fails to understand what is the real objective of life and living.

Finally in the old age he is disturbed by the inferoility and infirmity of old age when again he fails to think about life beyond the body.Thus not realizing the life and its objective spending and finishing one's life wastefully are many.

Due to one's karmic deeds the jive gets again and again born and it dies. The jive that gets both in this world for a short time and dies at young age of five or so is due to the sins committed by the jive. Only the one who has done misdeeds gets born and dies within a short life span again and again. There is no count for no. Of times he gets born and dies.

If a person has accumulated good karma in previous life and lived with good conduct, has done charities with a compassionate heart, and when such a person is born again in this mortal world, he gets to live with his wife and children for long and gets to lead a good dharmic life and then he also gets a chance to reach a good world later.

Oh! Vinadeya! After conceivement if the fetus gets aborted in between then following should be done
If the month of abortion is first month, the mother of the child should abstain from touching anyone for one day.
If the month of abortion is second month, the mother of the child should abstain from touching anyone for two days.
If the month of abortion is the third month, the mother of the child should abstain from touching anyone for three days and so on.

The father is not bounded by the rule. If the child gets properly born on 10th month, however if it dies in 3 days then in the name of the dead child some curd rice and milk should be given to small children around that place.

Also if the child dies in three to five years' similar food distribution should be done.
Even if the child dies within a month of its birth, the rites should be done as per the caste rules as well milk and `payas' should be given to children around in liquid form.

As persons born in this earth are sure to die and the dead person will be again born is also sure, it is important to try not to take another birth but reach birth and death less world, a blissful state.

However if a jive not trying for that not living a life of good conduct, doing charity and wastes its life time in wasteful adharmic activities then it may be again born in one of the four castes but as per the adharmic ways it will suffer in not getting even one proper meal. It may get born to a pauper and may live an ignoble, poverty stricken life.

Oh! Vinadeya! It would be better to do karma's aiming in not getting another birth at all which is ridden with pleasure and pain. He should not even aim for a birth in a higher caste, to be ruler of the whole world, to be a learned pandit knowing all sastras.

All those wishes of better rebirth pales in front of a reaching a world filled with bliss having no pangs of birth and death and living a life filled with ignorance as well pleasures and pain alternatively.

The one who does pilgrimage to holy places, having purity of mind, does not resort to cheating and lies, who cultivates to speak sweat words full of humility is bound to reap fruits of his good deeds.

A person having lot of wealth but does not give anything to charity is bound to be born as a poor person in the next janma. Hence it is very important for a person to do dhaan and dharma as per his wealth and strength.

IX

CHILDREN, GRAND CHILDREN AND KARMA

Sriman Narayana murthy addressed further Lord Garuda

Oh! Kasi putra! Apart from what is being told, hear further about the rites to be done for children and grandchildren. The jive which is born in this world dies as per the karmas done in the last janma (birth).

If the fetus dies with in the womb no rites need be done. If a child is born and dies within five years, the rites have to be done as per prescribed in the sastras and to the children around food, milk and payas has to be given. On the 10th day and 12th day of the child's death the rites can be done as told in the sastras.

For a five year old child's death there need not be done Vrishorchanam and special dhanna's. However whether the person dies as a young child, a young lad or an old person the udhaka kumbha dhanam has to be definitely to be done.

If a child less than three years dies, it has to be buried inside the mud. A child who completes 24 month and dies on 25th month onwards, It should be burnt by a pyre and cremated by fire.

A person who is born, for six months is considered an infant, for three years a young child, oill six years a young lad, oill nine years an young youth and for sixteen years a Brahma Chari, thus tells the sastras.

A person born in lower caste should not wear the sacred thread. Only persons born in Brahmin, kshatriya and vaisya caste can wear sacred thread.

If a child dies in five years of age either wearing sacred thread or not, than not much mantras have to be told to perform his rites. However ten days pinda has to be offered for the departed soul. For the young child of five years since his attachment with his body, the affection to the parents and involvement with other material things is limited hence the rites and mantras recited are also limited.

However if the child is above 5 yrs to 12 yrs or completes 12 yrs and dies then it is necessary to do Vishnorchanam but there is no need to do sapandhikaranam.

The pindam should be offered where cooked rice could be mixed with milk, curd and jaggery. The charity of a pot, umbrella, lamp etc can be done. If it is not done, in the next birth he will be born as a tree and that tree may be used to make a chitsle, which may be used to pound rice.

If shradhas like `ahodhista' are done wearing sacred thread on the left side, the dead person will get born in the next janma in a good family and live for a long life. He will get a good son.

It is true one's own soul gets born as one's son. That is why if the son dies his father should do the rites and if father dies the son should do the rites. The Vedas tell one becomes one's own son.

There is only one sun and only one moon. If a series of pots are kept filled with water and if one looks at their reflections in each pot in the day time the same sun will be seen.

In the nighttime, the same moon will be seen. In the same way the same person is born to one's self as many sons. That is why many of the children look like one's father has similar intellect, discipline and characteristics.

However a blind person does not get a blind child, a dumb person does not be get a dumb child, a deaf person does not beget a deaf child. Thus generally good characteristic of the father will fit a child born to him than otherwise.

Garuda Bhagawan then worshipped the Parama pitha and addressed him as `Jagannatha', and told ` It is said in the sastras there are 10 kinds of son one can have.

Like one can have one's own son, or it can be a son born to one's wife or one can have a son through a prostitute and such other kinds too. Can the son born out of a prostitute do rites to his father? Further if such a son does for him rites, can he reach a good state and good world after accepting these rites? If a person has only daughters and the daughter also does not have sons than who soill do the rites for him? Kindly explain and inform me clearly these doubts of mine.

On hearing these God Narayana who is always compassionate to his bhaktis looked at Garuda and told thus.

Oh! King of birds! If a person sees the face of the son born to him through his legal wife, he does not have to see the hell called `puth' after his death.

If a properly wedded husband and wife get a son, the ancestors of his lineage become very happy. If a person begets 10 sons, out of them only the eldest son gets the right to do the rites of his father. Rather he is duty bound to do it. The other 9 sons are entitled to help their father for the life in this earth but have no rights and duties to help their father for the onward journey. They can at the most do some lesser rites and shradha for the departed.

If a person dies after he sees his grandson, then he get blessed and his reaching a good world after death increases. If he dies after sighting his great grandchild, he will reach soill better state.

If a person gets a son in law without accepting any money for his daughter's marriage and thus gets opportunity to do charity of his daughter to a true gentleman and when they beget a son in their union, that son will have the strength to help in crossing his lineages to a good state after death for 21 generations. A son born thus alone will have the complete right to do the rites to one's parents.

If one had a son from one's lover He can do only limited rites for his father. However if he insists on doing all the rites, the person who dies and the dead person both will reach hell.

However such a son can do shradh every year for his father. But he is not supposed to do anything for his father's ancestors. He can do charities keeping his dead father in mind. But he is not supposed to give food for the Brahmins.

He can however supply raw rice and other things for making food. But he should never think of himself to be like the dead persons own son and do rites.

The son who has been born by proper means can do pilgrimage for the welfare of the departed. Thinking about one's pitur (ancestors) he can do `shradh' in `anna rupa' (food form). In form of tortoise, in form of `hiranya'.

However the lover's son if he does pilgrimage, he cannot do shrada in anna rupa (food form) but he can do in other forms.

In sudra sect if any one does shrada in anna form, the one who does shradha, the Brahmin who partakes the food and the piturs (ancestors) all will reach hell.

Oh! King of birds, a child born out of a union of a Brahmin and a lower caste man, a Brahmin lady and a sanyasi, union of brothers and sisters will become `chandala' (men destined to do lowly jobs).

When a person marries a lady in one's own caste and gets a son from that union, that son alone is an exalted one. Hence people should strive to get `satputras' for taking care of oneself and one's ancestors.

X

SAPANDIKARANAM AND SATIPATIKAL

Garuda gave his thankful oblations after Bhagawan explaining who is entitled to do piturkarma and further started his entireties,

Oh! Jagannatha! When the rites called `sapandikaranam' should be done in the name of the dead person? What are the benefits the dead person obtains by doing sapandikaranam? What state will he obtain? How is it possible to join the recently dead one to his ancestors who had been dead long back through pindam? If they are joined what state they both will obtain?

If the husband is alive and the wife dies how to do sapandikaranam for her? All these you must tell me and explain for the understanding and goodness of the entire society.

For that Lord Kesava who is the beginning and end of all beings started telling.

Oh! The son of Vinutha, for the one who left this earthly life all rites should be done as written in the sastras and sapandikaranam also to be done and through this his pinda should be joined with his ancestors of his group who have already been dead.

If it is done so, he will get relieved of his pretha form and get joined with his ancestors.

The sapandikaranam can be done on the 12th day after the person dies or on the 3rd paksham or else on the 6th month after he is dead.

If the father is dead and the son should do rites for him but sapandikaranam is not done and later the son gets married, only after doing sapandikaranam he must consummate with his wife.

Since the person who passed away will remain in pretha atma oill sapandikaranam is done, the person who did rites will have the dosha.

Hence he should not do any auspicious acts. Only after joining the pindas during sapandikaranam the pretha form gets relieved and the dead will join the piturs and be happy.

Since the body is impermanent and anything can besiege the person doing rites it will be more proper to do sapandikaranam on 12th day itself. After doing sapandikaranam for the ancestors of three generations, shradam has to be done. If sodasham and sapandikaranam are done the dead person will shed definitely his pretha form and join the piturs and become happy.

If a person had given his daughter in marriage without accepting any money from the groom's party later if he dies the son in laws gotra should be taken and all kriyas should be done. However if like selling a piece of flesh the father had taken money for marrying off his daughter then the son in laws gotra need not be taken.

If a son is not there then his youngest brother or eldest brother can do the rites. If the brothers after parting the father's property are living separately then his wife can do the karma.

If the dead person does not have a son, brother or their sons or even wife, then the dead person gotra relatives (dayadi) can do rites. If dayadhi is also not there, if he has students taught by him then they can do the karmas.

If none of these people are there than the purohit himself can do. If four or five brothers are there out of them one brother alone has a son, then the other brothers can also claim him as their own son. It is similar to if a person has many wives and only one wife has child, then that child can be claimed by other wives also as their own child.

If the father dies before upanayanam is done for the son, soill that son alone has to do the rites. If a lady does not have son, her husband has to do the rites for her.

If during sapandikaranam either due to ignorance if all the piturdevas (three line of ancestors) are not invited and appeased and only for the dead person 'pinda' is given and rites are performed than the one who is doing the rites, the dead person as well the purohidhar will reach the hell.

Even if many are there for the dead person, only the same person has to do all the rites for one year. Apart from daily shradham, in a pot 'punal' has to be filled and 'udhakakumbha dhanam' has to be done. If all the homas are done without fail the person who dies will alight the pushpaka vimanam and reach a good world.

If the grand father is alive and father dies, sapandikaranam should not be done for him after the grandfather dies and after doing sapandikaranam to him then for the father it should be done.

If father and father's mother are alive and a person's mother dies then for the mother sapandikaranam should not be done. After both of them die and sapandikaranam is to be done for them then alone it should be done for the mother.

Oh! Vinadeya however these rules are not absolute. If a woman considers her husband as the god and she sees and lives with a endearing bhakti to her husband and after his death, in the pyre made to burn his body, she also annihilates her body, then she will reach a good state better than others in the earth.

Even if she has done some or many sins, by the act of sacrificing her body along with her husbands with a feeling of bhakti, she becomes a great punya doer. This act will erase her husband's sins too and both will become blessed to live in heaven together for a long time. For such a parent the son has to do one sapandikaranam for both. However rites and charities should be done separately for both of them and pindam should be offered.

As how when a maligned gold bar is put in fire, the fire won't harm the gold but only will remove the blemish in the gold, same way the fire will burn only the body of the women who jumps into the pyre with her husband but won't bring any harm to herself.

A women who relinquishes her mother, father, son, brother, sister and other relatives, her house and other material things which she has been attached to and firmly thinks her husband alone is the god she sees and decided to sacrifice her life along with her husbands with great bhakti is indeed a great punya atma.

She will stay with her husband for three and half crore deva varsha (yrs) in the devaloka with lot of bliss Later she will get born in a exalted yogis family also her husband will get born in another such good family and again obtain the same person as husband and live a good life.

However if a woman betrays her husband and develops illicit relationship with another person and by his prompting ridicules her own husband and brings ill fame to one's own birth family, she will get a female ghost form and reach hell.

The one who remain faithful to her husband whether he is good person or bad person, intelligent or stupid and thinks of him alone whether he is alive or dead is the one proper in her conduct and benefits by the same.

However the person who thinks lowly of her husband and roams around as per her whims is looked down by others who condemn her telling ` Is she a woman of any character?' and will in the next janma marry a very bad person. She will be repeatedly get punished and admonished by him and will suffer in untold ways.

If the husband does worship of gods, does hospitality to guests, undertakes vrathas and penances then the wife also should follow these and help her husband in these matters. As how it is the dharma and duty of the lower caste to serve the higher caste persons, same way it is the duty of wife to serve her husband in all ways.

This dharma is applicable to all caste persons. The one who thinks the husband is god one sees, after she dies will be born in a high caste house and will obtain a good person as her husband. She will give birth to good children and bring fame to the father who gave birth to her and the husband who marries her and will leave life as a sumangali, that is when husband is soill alive and reach an exalted world.

Oh! Kasi putra! The dead person after being dead as not to undergo any suffering but to get all the happiness let me tell you another matter, listen

After doing sapandikaranam on the 12th day, for one year daily shradh has to be done. For whoever daily shradh is done not only he but the one doing shradh also will receive a lot of good benefits thus told Lord Narayana and blessed Garuda with his words of wisdom.

XI

CHILDREN, GRANDCHILDREN AND KARMACHILDREN,

Sriman Narayana murthy addressed further Lord Garuda

Oh! Kasi putra! Apart from what is being told, hear further about the rites to be done for children and grandchildren. The jive which is born in this world dies as per the karmas done in the last janma (birth).

If the fetus dies with in the womb no rites need be done. If a child is born and dies within five years, the rites have to be done as per prescribed in the sastras and to the children around food, milk and payas has to be given. On the 10th day and 12th day of the child's death the rites can be done as told in the sastras.

For a five year old child's death there need not be done Vrishorchanam and special dhanna's. However whether the person dies as a young child, a young lad or an old person the udhaka kumbha dhanam has to be definitely to be done.

If a child less than three years dies, it has to be buried inside the mud. A child who completes 24 month and dies on 25th month onwards, It should be burnt by a pyre and cremated by fire.

A person who is born, for six months is considered an infant, for three years a young child, oill six years a young lad, oill nine years an young youth and for sixteen years a Brahma Chari, thus tells the sastras.

A person born in lower caste should not wear the sacred thread. Only persons born in Brahmin, kshatriya and vaisya caste can wear sacred thread.

If a child dies in five years of age either wearing sacred thread or not, than not much mantras have to be told to perform his rites. However ten days pinda has to be offered for the departed soul. For the young child of five years since his attachment with his body, the affection to the parents and involvement with other material things is limited hence the rites and mantras recited are also limited.

However if the child is above 5 yrs to 12 yrs or completes 12 yrs and dies then it is necessary to do Vishnorchanam but there is no need to do sapandhikaranam.

The pindam should be offered where cooked rice could be mixed with milk, curd and jaggery. The charity of a pot, umbrella, lamp etc can be done. If it is not done, in the next birth he will be born as a tree and that tree may be used to make a chitsle, which may be used to pound rice.

If shradhas like `ahodhista' are done wearing sacred thread on the left side, the dead person will get born in the next janma in a good family and live for a long life. He will get a good son.

It is true one's own soul gets born as one's son. That is why if the son dies his father should do the rites and if father dies the son should do the rites. The Vedas tell one becomes one's own son.

There is only one sun and only one moon. If a series of pots are kept filled with water and if one looks at their reflections in each pot in the day time the same sun will be seen.

In the nighttime, the same moon will be seen. In the same way the same person is born to one's self as many sons. That is why many of the children look like one's father has similar intellect, discipline and characteristics.

However a blind person does not get a blind child, a dumb person does not be get a dumb child, a deaf person does not beget a deaf child. Thus generally good characteristic of the father will fit a child born to him than otherwise.

Garuda Bhagawan then worshipped the Parama pitha and addressed him as `Jagannatha', and told ` It is said in the sastras there are 10 kinds of son one can have.

Like one can have one's own son, or it can be a son born to one's wife or one can have a son through a prostitute and such other kinds too. Can the son born out of a prostitute do rites to his father? Further if such a son does for him rites, can he reach a good state and good world after accepting these rites? If a person has only daughters and the daughter also does not have sons than who soill do the rites for him? Kindly explain and inform me clearly these doubts of mine.

On hearing these God Narayana who is always compassionate to his bhaktis looked at Garuda and told thus.

Oh! King of birds! If a person sees the face of the son born to him through his legal wife, he does not have to see the hell called `puth' after his death.

If a properly wedded husband and wife get a son, the ancestors of his lineage become very happy. If a person begets 10 sons, out of them only the eldest son gets the right to do the rites of his father. Rather he is duty bound to do it. The other 9 sons are entitled to help their father for the life in this earth but have no rights and duties to help their father for the onward journey. They can at the most do some lesser rites and shradha for the departed.

If a person dies after he sees his grandson, then he get blessed and his reaching a good world after death increases. If he dies after sighting his great grandchild, he will reach soill better state.

If a person gets a son in law without accepting any money for his daughter's marriage and thus gets opportunity to do charity of his daughter to a true gentleman and when they beget a son in their union, that son will have the strength to help in crossing his lineages to a good state after death for 21 generations. A son born thus alone will have the complete right to do the rites to one's parents.

If one had a son from one's lover He can do only limited rites for his father. However if he insists on doing all the rites, the person who dies and the dead person both will reach hell.

However such a son can do shradh every year for his father. But he is not supposed to do anything for his father's ancestors. He can do charities keeping his dead father in mind. But he is not supposed to give food for the Brahmins.

He can however supply raw rice and other things for making food. But he should never think of himself to be like the dead persons own son and do rites.

The son who has been born by proper means can do pilgrimage for the welfare of the departed. Thinking about one's pitur (ancestors) he can do `shradh' in `anna rupa' (food form). In form of tortoise, in form of `hiranya'.

However the lover's son if he does pilgrimage, he cannot do shrada in anna rupa (food form) but he can do in other forms.

In sudra sect if any one does shrada in anna form, the one who does shradha, the Brahmin who partakes the food and the piturs (ancestors) all will reach hell.

Oh! King of birds, a child born out of a union of a Brahmin and a lower caste man, a Brahmin lady and a sanyasi, union of brothers and sisters will become `chandala' (men destined to do lowly jobs).

When a person marries a lady in one's own caste and gets a son from that union, that son alone is an exalted one. Hence people should strive to get `satputras' for taking care of oneself and one's ancestors.

SAPANDIKARANAM AND SATIPATIKAL

Garuda gave his thankful oblations after Bhagawan explaining who is entitled to do piturkarma and further started his entireties,

Oh! Jagannatha! When the rites called `sapandikaranam' should be done in the name of the dead person? What are the benefits the dead person obtains by doing sapandikaranam? What state will he obtain? How is it possible to join the recently dead one to his ancestors who had been dead long back through pindam? If they are joined what state they both will obtain?

If the husband is alive and the wife dies how to do sapandikaranam for her? All these you must tell me and explain for the understanding and goodness of the entire society.

For that Lord Kesava who is the beginning and end of all beings started telling.

Oh! The son of Vinutha, for the one who left this earthly life all rites should be done as written in the sastras and sapandikaranam also to be done and through this his pinda should be joined with his ancestors of his group who have already been dead.

If it is done so, he will get relieved of his pretha form and get joined with his ancestors.

The sapandikaranam can be done on the 12th day after the person dies or on the 3rd paksham or else on the 6th month after he is dead.

If the father is dead and the son should do rites for him but sapandikaranam is not done and later the son gets married, only after doing sapandikaranam he must consummate with his wife.

Since the person who passed away will remain in pretha atma oill sapandikaranam is done, the person who did rites will have the dosha.

Hence he should not do any auspicious acts. Only after joining the pindas during sapandikaranam the pretha form gets relieved and the dead will join the piturs and be happy.

Since the body is impermanent and anything can besiege the person doing rites it will be more proper to do sapandikaranam on 12th day itself. After doing sapandikaranam for the ancestors of three generations, shradam has to be done. If sodasham and sapandikaranam are done the dead person will shed definitely his pretha form and join the piturs and become happy.

If a person had given his daughter in marriage without accepting any money from the groom's party later if he dies the son in laws gotra should be taken and all kriyas should be done. However if like selling a piece of flesh the father had taken money for marrying off his daughter then the son in laws gotra need not be taken.

If a son is not there then his youngest brother or eldest brother can do the rites. If the brothers after parting the father's property are living separately then his wife can do the karma.

If the dead person does not have a son, brother or their sons or even wife, then the dead person gotra relatives (dayadi) can do rites. If dayadhi is also not there, if he has students taught by him then they can do the karmas.

If none of these people are there than the purohit himself can do. If four or five brothers are there out of them one brother alone has a son, then the other brothers can also claim him as their own son. It is similar to if a person has many wives and only one wife has child, then that child can be claimed by other wives also as their own child.

If the father dies before upanayanam is done for the son, soill that son alone has to do the rites. If a lady does not have son, her husband has to do the rites for her.

If during sapandikaranam either due to ignorance if all the piturdevas (three line of ancestors) are not invited and appeased and only for the dead person `pinda' is given and rites are performed than the one who is doing the rites, the dead person as well the purohidhar will reach the hell.

Even if many are there for the dead person, only the same person has to do all the rites for one year. Apart from daily shradham, in a pot `punal' has to be filled and `udhakakumbha dhanam' has to be done. If all the homas are done without fail the person who dies will alight the pushpaka vimanam and reach a good world.

If the grand father is alive and father dies, sapandikaranam should not be done for him after the grandfather dies and after doing sapandikaranam to him then for the father it should be done.

If father and father's mother are alive and a person's mother dies then for the mother sapandikaranam should not be done. After both of them die and sapandikaranam is to be done for them then alone it should be done for the mother.

Oh! Vinadeya however these rules are not absolute. If a woman considers her husband as the god and she sees and lives with a endearing bhakti to her husband and after his death, in the pyre made to burn his body, she also annihilates her body, then she will reach a good state better than others in the earth.

Even if she has done some or many sins, by the act of sacrificing her body along with her husbands with a feeling of bhakti, she becomes a great punya doer. This act will erase her husband's sins too and both will become blessed to live in heaven together for a long time. For such a parent the son has to do one sapandikaranam for both. However rites and charities should be done separately for both of them and pindam should be offered.

As how when a maligned gold bar is put in fire, the fire won't harm the gold but only will remove the blemish in the gold, same way the fire will burn only the body of the women who jumps into the pyre with her husband but won't bring any harm to herself.

A women who relinquishes her mother, father, son, brother, sister and other relatives, her house and other material things which she has been attached to and firmly thinks her husband alone is the god she sees and decided to sacrifice her life along with her husbands with great bhakti is indeed a great punya atma.

She will stay with her husband for three and half crore deva varsha (yrs) in the devaloka with lot of bliss Later she will get born in a exalted yogis family also her husband will get born in another such good family and again obtain the same person as husband and live a good life.

However if a woman betrays her husband and develops illicit relationship with another person and by his prompting ridicules her own husband and brings ill fame to one's own birth family, she will get a female ghost form and reach hell.

The one who remain faithful to her husband whether he is good person or bad person, intelligent or stupid and thinks of him alone whether he is alive or dead is the one proper in her conduct and benefits by the same.

However the person who thinks lowly of her husband and roams around as per her whims is looked down by others who condemn her telling ` Is she a woman of any character?' and will in the next janma marry a very bad person. She will be repeatedly get punished and admonished by him and will suffer in untold ways.

If the husband does worship of gods, does hospitality to guests, undertakes vrathas and penances then the wife also should follow these and help her husband in these matters. As how it is the dharma and duty of the lower caste to serve the higher caste persons, same way it is the duty of wife to serve her husband in all ways.

This dharma is applicable to all caste persons. The one who thinks the husband is god one sees, after she dies will be born in a high caste house and will obtain a good person as her husband. She will give birth to good children and bring fame to the father who gave birth to her and the husband who marries her and will leave life as a sumangali, that is when husband is soill alive and reach an exalted world.

Oh! Kasi putra! The dead person after being dead as not to undergo any suffering but to get all the happiness let me tell you another matter, listen

After doing sapandikaranam on the 12th day, for one year daily shradh has to be done. For whoever daily shradh is done not only he but the one doing shradh also will receive a lot of good benefits thus told Lord Narayana and blessed Garuda with his words of wisdom

XII

THE SIGNIFICANCE OF OIL AND DARPA (A KIND OF GRASS)

Garuda worshipped Tirumal with great humility and told `Sarvesa! You have been telling all these important matters very shortly. But I have some small doubts which I would like to clear before starting to do the rites.

Why the ground is swept with cow dung before starting the rites? Why Oil and darba grass are being used while doing the pitur karmas? Once you told a person who leaves his life while lying in the bed and sleeping and the one who stays in an upper storey and leaves his life will not reach a good state? If that is so the person who is about to die should be where and which manner he should die to reach a good loka?

How the charities have to be done? What are the benefits of these charities? For all these please give me the answers and explain the matter clearly.

The most compassionate Sri Purushotham looked at Garuda and started replying, Vainadeya! You asked a good question! I will tell in detail that entire one has to do for a dead person, listen carefully.

For a person not given birth to a son there may not be happiness in any world. A person who desires to get happiness in this world and the world he goes to should definitely do penance and good karma to get a good son.

If he does not do dharma and penance his wives womb does not get filled with a good child. Even if a child gets conceived it will get aborted before its full tenure of 10 months. If the fetus get destroyed and aborted the man won't get a good state. The one who has done good deeds alone will get a good son and reap goodness from all the worlds he reaches.

Vainadeya! Before doing karma's a place has to be ear marked. It has to be cleaned well and swept by cow dung and then the rites are to be done. Without cleaning the place if the rites are done, then bhutas, prethas, pisasus and demons may invade the place and obstruct the karmas and may not allow it to get completed.

If the rites are started in a clean place then devas will come there and help in completing the karmas. However if it is thought, after all he is a dead person what if his rites are done anywhere, in any unclean place, so thinking if the rites are done then the dead person may not get full benefit of the rites and not only that he may reach hell as a result.

`Oil' this condiment has come out of sweat. Hence this is a very pure substance. It is of 2 types. Black oil and while oil. Any kind of oil if given with charity it will augur well.

During shradha period if black oil is used the pitur will get more satisfied. The darpa grass initially arrived from the sky. At one end of the darpa grass is Brahma; the other end is Shiva and in between is Sri Hari. Without this darpa grass shardam and other karmas should not be done.

A darpa once used can again can be re used. The ekadasi vrath, the leaf tulasi, Bhagavat Gita, cow, bhakti for a Brahmin, the feet of Sri Hari, all these act as good boats for crossing the ocean of samsara.

The one who is about to die should spread darba grass in the ground swept well with cow dung and sit or lie down on it. Holding darba grass and tulsi leaves if he chants the name of me, the Lord Narayana and die, then he will reach the rarest place, my abode and remain happily there, filled with bliss.

The one who is to die should not lie face down on his stomach in the darba grass. He should lie only face up. Along with tulsi leaves he must do lot of charities to the people around before his death. In that to give charity of salt is good. The salt originally came from Vishnu loka. Hence its importance is high. The dying person or in the name of the dying person if salt is given as charity he may reach swarga' thus told Lord Tirumal.

DIFFERENT KINDS OF CHARITIES

Tirumal started telling to Garuda `garuda! , I will tell you now the method of doing charities and benefit accrued by doing such charities.

Among the dhanas the cotton or cloth dhana is one the good ones. It is also called at times as the mahadhana. The Brahmins who live by Brahmin order who learn scriptures, get proficiency in the Vedas, wear the sacred thread which is woven by cotton threads, when these punya atmas live in the world it is cotton cloth which help them to cover their naked bodies as well protect them from heat and cold. This cotton and cloth made of it thus gains significance.

If cotton and cotton cloth is given as charity, Lord Indra and devas will be satisfied.

The one who does such a charity will reach shivalok after death. There he will stay for long time, then later will be born in earth with a good form, beautiful body, having all good qualities.

He will be born as a strong person, as a king and ruler of lot of land, gifted with long life. He will get name and fame and later reach swarga after death.

If charity of oil, cow, land, gold, grains etc are done then great sins will be washed off. Both oil charity and cow charity are exalted ones. These charities will annihilate very bad sins. Hence these charities should not be given to ordinary Brahmin. Only very disciplined Brahmins it should be given.

All charities should not be given to closely related ones and one's own family members. Though they can be given some charities but the main one's should be given to outsiders or else the charities will remain in the family only.

The best time to do charities is when the jive is about to die of is just dead. The time after eclipse is also a good time to do charities.

Oh! Vinadeya for any person it will be better to do charities when he is alive, in a happy frame of mind and living well. If such a person has a son then it would be better to inform the son and take his permission and then do the dhanam.

When a person is about to die if he does charity or arranges to do charity of oil, iron, salt, cotton, cereals, gold, land, cow etc then these will be very beneficial to him for onward journey.

If iron and oil are given then lord Yama dharma will become very happy. If salt dhanam is done the dying person wont feel scared about Lord Yama. If cotton charity is done then he wont feel afraid of Yama duthas.

The charity of gold and cow has the power to annihilate all sins. This I suppose I had told before itself.

The one who is about to die if he meditates on Me, repeats My name and dies, he will reach the vaikunta, abode of Myself, the Tirumal and live there blissfully for ever.

After death of one's father instead of doing Gaya shradh, if one remains near one's father and does charities and do dharmic acts that will fetch better results.

The weapons of kalan are knife, iron rod, muslam, and kudaram. All his weapons are made of iron. Thus when a person dies if iron is given in charity Lord Yama will become happy, thus I told isn't it? This iron charity gives such protection to the dying soul that even yama dutas will approach the soul with great respect. This especially satisfies the Yamaduthas.

Vainadeya! In a jive's body parts, right from head to foot all the devas, including Lord of devas Indra, Lord SriKrishna are all abiding in him.

The father, mother, Guru, relations are all none but Sri Lord Vishnu himself for the jives.

You must have heard the words of grace` Sarvam Vishnumayam jagath' (The entire world is Lord Vishnu in different forms everywhere). This is very true.

The land, earth, water, fire, wind, sky, gold, cereals, honey, ghee, cows, yagnas, the Brahmin, the multitudes devas and Indra deva, everything and everyone are none but Vishnu.

The one who gives, the one who takes, all entities, all jives are not but we alone that are Lord Vishnu Himself. The jives as per the previous karmas they have done, according to the papa and punyas, their mind get diverted to good and bad deeds.

These acts are done by us to ourselves.
The one who does good deeds reaches heaven and the one who does bad deeds reaches hell.

XIII
THE IMPORTANCE OF CHARITIES AND THE WAY THE LIFE LEAVES THE BODY

Lord Sriman Narayana, who is the cause of the whole world, looked at Garuda and told `Vainadeya! The one who worships me and does charity in the holy places will obtain lot of punya's by those acts.

If land is given in charity in name of the dead soul, as how much deep the land is that many years the jive will stay in Swarga loka'.
If horse is given on charity the jive will ride in a horse and reach the good world. Enroute he will not be troubled by

thorns and other obstructive things.

If he gives charity of umbrella than a shaded path will be allotted to him to go to Yamapuri. Even if it rains he won't be troubled with that. If charity of lamp is done than on a darkened path he will be shown light.

If a person dies in Krithika, masi, Ippasi months or in thitdi like chaturdasi and pournami than it is advisable to give charity of lamp on the day of his death itself.

If deepa dhana (charity of lamp) is done from the day of his death for one year every day then he will reach Yamapuri without any obstacles as pits and rough patches etc. If anyone else is there of his family who has died, they can also be helped to reach a good world and a good state.

The significance of deepa dhana cannot be underestimated. If deepa is kept in a temple it should be kept either north facing or east facing. When the dhana is done the lamp should be burning against the face of the person and not facing him.

A person born as human being should die some time or else. This being a sure fact, a person can also do charities by himself to himself. A person who gives as charity a `asana' (a wooden sitting mat), a tali (copper dollar) and a food item made by himself to someone deserving, he will travel happily by a safe route to `paralok' after death.

Rice, oil, thirteen pots, a ring, umbrella, a fan, slippers all these should be definitely given on charity for persons after or before death. If horse, elephant etc. are given special punya will be accrued.

When a buffalo is given on charity it is better to give lot of things along with that, it will augur well. If betel leaves, betel nut (supari), flowers are given as charity the yamaduth will become happy and they may not trouble the jive.

If clothes are given as charity then the yamaduths who have grotesque looks, a heavy set black body like the overbearing black rain clouds, sharp bend canine teeth, over grown brown body hair and a huge fear producing look, will appear in good pleasant figure in front of the jive.

On hearing these Garuda further entreated Lord Hari and asked Oh! Saviour of humble one's in distress, do please tell me how the life leaves the body?

On his plea the Lord who is the knowledge of all happenings started telling, Garuda! The life when it leaves the human body, leaves by his eyes, nose or by the holes of his hair follicles.

For the wise one the life leaves from the top of the skull. After the life leaves the human body it becomes like a wooden piece. Later the lifeless body made of five elements become one with the respective elements in the universe.

The five elements are earth, water, fire, air and sky. It will meet its peer at the universe.

The six states of mind as desire, anger, greed, attraction, intoxication and `macharyam' and five Gyanedriyam stay inside the human body locked with one another in a subtle hidden form.

When the life leaves the body all these freezes in to the mind. Then chetna or mind due to his karma's gets another janma or life

As how a person living in an old house after getting wealth makes a new house and goes to stay there same way the jive who has done punyas after completing one's life time, will again enter another body having all indriyas in good condition and continues to enjoy life as per his past karmas.

The unwanted waste products like urine, stools, the unproductive imaginations and the body along with the nerves, bones muscles get destroyed. The body is later burnt or buried and thus gets annihilated.

Thus this human body is highly impermanent. Oh! Garuda! This is the way a human being dies.

The body is an organism fitted with five indriyas as well having emotions like desire, anger, love, greed, moha, hostility etc. Also in this body resides all the devas who belong to all the worlds.

THE STORY OF DEVENDRAN GETTING ENTICED, MONTHLY MENSES, RELATIONSHIP BETWEEN MARRIED COUPLES, GROWTH OF FETUS

Garuda worshipped Paramapada nadan and told ` Oh! Protector of the entire world!

The human body, which is made up of skin, nerves, bone, blood, muscle, head, hands, legs, tongue, nose, sex organs, nail, hair etc. looks like a magic box isn't it? Please tell me the secret behind the making of such a complicated organism.'

The Paramdama who is the maker and protector of many worlds looked at the king of birds Garuda and told, Oh! Son of Kasyapa muni the question you asked is a good and important question, I will tell you,

`The women who are afflicted with menses should stay out of the living quarters for four days, I will tell you how this four day menses course started for women.

Once long time before, Lord Indra was in his palace and enjoying in his royal chamber the dance of beautiful deva kanyas, who were dancing to the melodious music played by gandarvas.

He was completely immersed in the dance and music. That time the Deva guru Brahaspathi (Lord Jupiter) came there. Lord Indra failed to notice the arrival of his guru and thus failed to do the welcoming respects due to him. He was completely enticed by the charms of the dancing girls.

His guru felt much belittled by the lack of welcome and his student ignoring him under the attraction of the dancing girls. He in anguish left the place after a while.

As Lord Indra failed to respect his very honourable guru, gradually he started sliding to bad times. His wealth started decreasing. Seeing such dismal happening around him, soon Lord Indra by enquiry and investigation realized he is going through such misfortune due to the disrespect he showed to his guru.

Repenting on his acts of omission Lord Indra went in search of his guru Brahaspathi. He could not find him in his place or anywhere else. He returned with a confused and disturbed state of mind to the four-faced Lord Brahma and reported him what ever happened.

Lord Brahma thought about it and contemplated and told Indra ` Indra! The mistake you did is indeed is a fault done by you. The punishment meted out to you for that by your teacher is a correct one. Hence your teacher has left you and gone.

Till your guru comes back you require a teacher isn't it? There is a elderly respectable person called Duveshta. His son is one called Vichuva varavan. He is a leader and a good disciplined person. He is a vidvan and highly knowledgeable person. You can make him your guru,' thus he blessed him.

Indra accepted the advice given by Lord Brahma and decided to make Vichvavaravan his teacher and invited him to Indra lok as his teacher. Vichvavaravan also accepted the invitation and took the place of Lord Brahaspati.

After a while Lord Indra wanted to do a yagna. He expressed his wish to his new guru. The yagna started. However the guru did not have a pure mind and intention. In the course of the yagna the guru told avaha mantra to his ancestors belonging to rakshsa kula.

Lord Indra soon came to know the betrayal act of his new guru. He rose in anger wielded his powerful weapon vajraaytha, cut and rolled down the 3 heads of his new guru. Though the guru died immediately as he possessed powers due to his austere penances his three heads, the one used for drinking soma rasa became a buffalo, the one used for drinking sura rasa became house sparrow, the one used for taking anna (rice) became kicahli bird.

Though Vichva varavan was a rakshasa since he was a guru and killing a guru is a very heinous act. Lord Indra came under the spell of Brahmahathi dosha.

The devas, the subjects of deva loka seeing their leader caught by this dosha tried various methods of parihara (repentance) to get him out of this dosha.

They requested the earth, water and women to take some of the dosha on them and relieve their leader out from that. The compassionate mother earth, cool waters and motherly women agreed to accept the dosha and suffer so that Lord Indra can come out of it and conduct his duties.

However they asked the devas how they should come out of this dosha after a time. For that the devas said, ` in water the dosha will come out as foam or lather. In earth it will come out as salt. In women it will come out as monthly menses.

Then they asked ` we who take and suffer the dosha, will we obtain anything good from it? For that the devas told` Anything which undergoes pain will definitely yield sweet fruits' ` Is it not true the earth which gets dug alone get filled with water.

Water, which is drained alone, gets again filled with water. Wood which is cut alone will again give out more shoots, same way a women who goes through the menses will later enjoy with her husband and conceive to get children."

Thus the brahmahathi which and taken hold of Lord Indra left him and took hold of the bodies of women, earth and water. Thus the women by getting monthly menses bore the dosha and started going through it every month.

Hence such a women who is under the spell of the dosha for 4 days in a month should not be seen by elders. If they see her they also can get some of the dosha. The one who gets periods will on first day look like a chandala women. Second day will be like a one who has done Brahmahathi third day will look like a washerwomen. Fourth day after having a head wash will become somewhat pure. On fifth day she will be pure and fit to do all house and family work.

From the sixth day onwards Till 18th day on even days and nights if union is done by the woman with her man a male child will be born. Hence a person wishing to get male child should join with one's wife on even days only. Then chances of a male child who is good in character, rich, dharmic and devoted to Lord Vishnu will be conceived.

Generally conceivement takes place from the 4th day to 8th day after the period starts. The fifth day after periods the women can drink`payas' and offers sweet items. They should avoid hot, pungent things.

The men should apply sandal wood paste and other pleasant auspicious things like flower, betel leaves should be had. Then in a happy frame of mind and with desire in heart they should have union with their wives.

If they unite like that by the union of sukla (the seed of man) and ova (the seed of women) conceivement takes place in the womb of woman and the fetus grows like a waxing moon gradually. The union takes place when the love god Manamathan and mind of the couple are in unity, the semen and ova which get released from the respective bodies of men and women unite.

If the semen of men is stronger than a male child will be conceived. If the strength of ova is more than a female child will be conceived. If both are equal than it will be a eunuch. (unisex)

If the women conceive, than on the 5th day of conceivement, in the womb or uterus a deepening will happen. By 14teen days it will get filled with fat and blood like a cushion. It increases in size. Further by 25th day it becomes a sizable proportion. By 1st month the `pancha bootha' (five elements) join the fetus lying in the cushioned womb.

On the second month the fetus gets the skin. On the third month it gets the nerves. On the fourth month it forms hair and outside form. On fifth moth end nose gets formed. On sixth month neck and head get properly formed. On seventh month the sex organs get formed. On eight month all organs and body gets formed and the jive enters the fetus. On ninth month the jive gets prana of purva janma karmas's from the muladara nadi containing the bud of all thought process. It gets saddened to get another janma and 10th month it gets born.

Vainadeya! The body made of pancha butha is made of five indriyas. It is decorated by 10 important nadis and ten vayus. The ten vayus are prana, apana, vyana, udhana, samana, naga, kurma, graga and devadatha.

Further this body made of six envelopes. They are sukram, bone, water, hair and blood.

The skin, bone, hair, muscle and nail are made from qualities of earth (mud). The saliva in the mouth, urine, semen, sweat, pus is all made from qualities of water.

Hunger, thirst, sleep, laziness, attraction are made from the qualities of fire.

Desire, anger, shyness, fear, covet ness, running, sit quietly without doing anything are the qualities of air.

Sound, thought, enquires, pride these are the qualities of sky. Ears, eyes, nose, tongue, skin all these five are gynaindriyas.

Ida , pingala, mula chakra these three are important nadis of the body. Gandari, gaja simmahi, puuzi, yachu, Alabhu, guru, vizakini these seven are body's important nadis.

The food and liquids the jive eats are taken by the vayu to the respective places in the body. Above the fire in the stomach is water and above that is annam. The fire in stomach is blown and flared by the vayu. In the entire body there are more than three crore hair openings, thirty two teeth, twenty nails, 27 crore head hair, one thousand bala muttan, hundred bala blood, ten bala medas, ten bala skin, twelve bala majjai (marrow) and three bala important blood.

Phlegm, stool, urine are also contained in the body. Whatever is in macrocosm is also found in the microcosm. Whatever is found in microcosm is found in the body.

The foot can be equated to atala lok. The ankle to vithala lok, the knee to sutala lok above the knee is nithala lok. The thigh is equated to tharthalam, the sex organ to rasathalam, the waist to pathalam. The navel to bhulok, the heart to swarga lok, the shoulder to maha lok, the face to jana lok, the forehead to thava lok, the head to satyalok.

The trikona near the muladara is termed to Merugiri, the lower triangle is termed as mantraparvatha, the right side of that is Himalayas, the north side is Nishepa mahaparvatham, and the south side is kunthamana parvatha.

The lines in the left palm are considered varuna parvatha. The bones are equated to naval island; the medas are equated to Sarahath Island. The muscle are equated to Sushi Island, the nerves are Crowchath Island. The skin is equated to Chanmadi Island. The hair group is equated to Platcha Island. The urine is considered salt sea. The water is considered Milk Sea. The phlegm is considered Sara sindu.

The marrow is considered to Chee Sea. The saliva to sea of sugarcane juice. The blood is considered as to curd sea. The air coming out of mouth is considered to sudodhka sindu.

In the body there are two main charkas. In nadha chakra lays the sun god, in bindu chakra lies the moon. In the eye lie mars planet, in heart lies planet mercury, in the words lie dev guru brhaspathi, in semen lies asura guru sukran, in navel lies Saturn, in face lies planet Rahu, in the legs lie planet ketu.

The human body contains 14 lokas, seven kalachala islands, nine grahas (planets). These are explained as above. When jive is in the womb itself Lord Brahma decides the for the jive how much life span is there, the talents of the jive, the amount of anger, yogam (fortune) and bhoga (experience) for the jive.

It also gets decided how the death of the jive will occur, the time and method of death also get decided as per the purva janma karmas done by the jive.

Hence at least to get long life, good talents, yoga (fortune), bhoga (experience) in the next janma the jive should do good deeds in this life thus the sastras are advising.

There is absolutely no doubt the jive obtains the fruits of the karma deeds of the previous janma in this life.

Garuda! The son of Kasyapa! All these I am telling you for the good will of the entire world. If you have anything more to ask you can ask that too. I will answer that, thus the compassionate lord blessed Garuda

XIV

YAMAS PALACE, CHITRAGUPTA'S MANDAP, RESULT OF PAPA ACTIONS.

Garuda thought for a while and gave his pranams to the Lord- Manivanna Perumal and told

`Oh! Sarvavyapi! Where is Yamapuri? How is the path to Yama loka looks like? Please tell me that in details 'thus he prayed.

Tirumal looked at Garuda and started telling` Vinadeya! I have told you about Yamapuri and the path leading to it once before.

As you are asking about it again, I will tell you the rest of it listen. The way to Yamapuri is a tough one. For some distance it will be very hot molten copper. After that for some time the way will be full of heavy thorns and hot cinders.

Then for some time the place will be unbearably biting cold. From Bhulok, Yamalok is 86,000-kada distances away. This I did mention before. All this way long the jive who has done papa (sins) will not even get a shade of a tree or little water available to quench its thirst.

For papa jive both Yamaloka and the way towards it will be very harsh. Garuda!
Now I will tell you about the appearance and ways of Yamalok. Listen! In the centre of south face and north face lays Yamapuri. It is strong like a diamond and constructed in such a way that it cannot be destroyed by devas and asuras. In the center of the city build as a Quadra square is the golden palace of Yamadharama Raja.

It is 100 yojana spacious, 25 yojanas in height, made of number of windows decorated by colourful flags, pearl and gem hangers, flower and auspicious leaf thoranas. There inside the palace is a decorated Divya mandap always echoing with dance and music recitals.

There Yamaduth can be seen with folded hands standing in one side and another side many kinds of diseases can be seen in there scary, grotesque forms.

In the center Yama dharma raja will be seen seated in a happy demonur but in a fiery form, which will scare anyone who sees him.

Close to it is Chitragupta's palace, which is about 25 yojana in length and breadth and 10 yojanas in height. It can also be seen as very ornamental decorated by pearls, gems and gold.

There in a Divya mandap Chitragupta can be seen seated. He will be seen writing the account of papa and punyas of all jives meticulously without leaving any detail. There won't be any mistake in the accounts written by

Chitra gupta.

In the east of Chitragupta's palace will be the graha (house) of the fever disease, in south is found graha of sala and vichari disease, west side will be found graha of indigestion, north side will be found the graha of stomach ache, southeast will be the graha of fainting, south west is found the graha of adchari disease, north east will be the graha of hysteria.

Thus for each disease separate grahas or houses are made. In these houses the diseases wait patiently to get yama's orders to act on the jive.

Garuda! In the south of yama's palace, the papa jives get tortured by yamakingaras in various ways.

Some jive can be seen beaten well by iron clubs. Some are beaten by sharp weapons. Some are put in oil churning mill and tortured. Some are tied in iron chain and heated in hot cinders.

Some till the others are heated and cooked in fire bowls. Vinadeya! There one can find men and women dolls made of copper are heated and made red-hot. Looking at jives who have enjoyed other women and prostitutes, the yamaduthas shout at them telling` papi's you did not think about dharma and disrespect but were bent on enjoying the women who were wedded to other men, just imagine what miseries this would have been to the other members who had been attached to the women like husband and parents.

Now the fruits of those miseries you also have to bear, thus telling those papa jives will be now joined with the lady dolls made of red hot molten metal. Oh! Sun of Vinitha! The men who enjoy a women other than his wedded wife and the women who enjoys a man other than her wedded husband are indeed given same punishment in Yamalok. Though such punishments are melted out some till people with good conducts are becoming rare in this earthly place.

Further in Yamalok the other forms of punishment are some jives are put in churning mill. As how sugar cane is crushed in the churner to make juice, same way the jive is churned till they cry out in great agony.

Some jives are pushed inside the deep end of the hell and made to suffer. The jives who have taken debt or loan which is not been paid back will be reprimanded harshly by yamaduths telling you scoundrel, you not only did not pay back your debts but tried to outwit your debtors by cheating them and were bad mouthing them.

Now get your punishment for your deeds, so saying they get thrashed well.

What is the purpose of telling the miseries undergone by papis? From the way persons live their lives it can be easily told this person is dharmic, this person is immoral, this person is destined to go to heaven, this person is destined to go to hell can be known.

It is for sure only persons who do dharmic deeds will go to swarga. Hence it is important everyone would go along the dharmic path, which is good for life here as well life in parlok.

SOME DHARMAS AND SOME POLLUTIONS

Tirumal looked compassionately at Garuda who is personification of veda form and told `Garuda, I will tell you some dharma's' listen.

Garuda! In kritha yuga it is good for human beings to do big penance. In Tritha yuga it is good for human beings to do dyana, in Dwapura yuga it is good for human beings to yagna. In kali yuga it is good for human beings to do dhanam (charities).

A person who is in grahstha ashram in which ever yuga he is, it is always good to help in making temples, pond, garden, choulteries to be hospitable to guests. These are some of the good acts, which will fetch him punya.

Other dharmic acts are- For a person staying with his family, if anybody of his clan dies he should do `tharpanam' (death rites) in the name of the dead. The dead person will become happy getting that offering.

After doing sanjyana all the dayathi(clan persons) should do tharpanam to the dead person. For the first three caste persons Brahmin, Kshatriya, vaisya, tharpanam can be done by shudhra. Kshatriya can do tharpanam for Brahmins. A Brahmin cannot do for other caste persons.

If along with a sudra's dead body if a Brahmin goes to the cremation ground, that Brahmin will get 3 days pollution or `aasousam' After 3 days that Brahmin has to take bath in holy rivers like Kaveri and become pure.

Whoever does karma for the dead person, he should not sleep in the soft cotton and other mattresses. He should lie in the floor or in the mat. The good deeds of the dead person only to be discussed and told. Prayers should be rendered to Lord Yama.

The dead person gets his pretha body after death only from the pindas offered in his name. Hence for 10 days the rites should be done without fail. If in proper order rites are not done the dead person will be troubled and feel miserable without his proper pretha body form.

As how a person trained in archery if he aims and throws an arrow his aim will reach the object without fail same way a good son when being properly aware of his duties and the rites he does and do the karmas for his parents, those benefits will reach the dead person without fail.

The dead jive will live for 3 days in water, 3 days in agni, 3 days in the sky and one day in his house in the form of `aavi' – ghost form.

On the first day, 3rd day, 5th day, 7th day, 9th day and 11th day nava shradham should be done. On the first day where ever tharpanam has been done, the other ten days on the same place rites has to be done.

The Brahmins, kshatriyas and vaishyas as per the number of days they have been asked to observe pollution that number for days they have to pinda tharpanam. It is very important.

In whichever thidhi the jive dies the same thidhi monthly rites (masikam) should be done. On the 11th day along with sweets and savouries food has to be cooked and should be emptied outside and bath has to be taken.

If a person dies after a lot of suffering and mental agony then Ahodhista shradam has to be done elaborately for him, then he will get peace.

This Ahodhista shradam should be done by kshatirya on 12th day and by vaisya on 15th day. If a parent die or a child is born, then one-month pollution has to be observed.

The clan persons of the dead person have pollution for 10 days. However in case he hears the news of death later then if it is in 3 months' time, he has to observe 3 days pollution. If he hears the news from 3 months to 1 year then he has to observe only one-day pollution.

If the news is heard after one year then as soon as the news is heard he has to take bath to clear him of pollution. This rule is applicable for all caste persons.

Vinadeya! I have told you before itself it is good to do charity of a bed. Now I will tell you how it can be done.

A cot has to be made in a good wood. The ends can be capped by gold or silver covers. It can decorated by pearl strings and flower garlands. Then a mat has to be spread on the floor.

This along with a lighted lamp, sandal wood flowers, betel leaves and nut and other scented articles, water, copper mangal sutra and different decorative things required for men and women can be kept over the cot.

Then puja can be done of navagrahas. All devas including Shiva and all devis including Parvathy, Goddess Lakshmi and God Narayana should be worshipped and seeked blessings.

Then seeking satisfaction of all heavenly entities it can be given in charity to a family man who is good.

XV

FINAL RITES BEFORE CREMATION

Garuda addressed Lord Murari, `Sarvesa! The one who has given birth to mother and her mother, the one who has given birth to father and his father, if all these people are alive and if father or mother dies then how their son has to join the pindas? Please tell me this to this humble one, thus he entreated.

For that Bhagawan told him thus, `Vainadeya! In mothers lineage and fathers lineage apart from those who are alive, further up three generations pindam, should be joined with the dead persons pindam.

The pindam eating piturs are many `Thyazakar three, lepahar three the one who sits to eat in pindam's food plate is one, thus in the lineage of father there are 10 persons. As one person dies the 4th generation person becomes

Thyasakar.

The third thyasakan (6th generation person) becomes Lepakan. The third lepakan, 10th generation person will be excluded from list henceforth. When the son does shradha the father becomes happy and gives a son to that son. If when shradam is done the piturs become satisfied the doer will be showered with lot of good things.

It is not proper to keep the body after the life has left it. The cremation has to be done immediately.

From avittam star onwards Till Revathi star the five days are not good days. For persons who die on these days the samaskara should not be done immediately. Only after these stars get passed the samskaras has to be done.

To clear the dosha (blemish) for the persons who have passed away in above stars and dhanishta star, which is also not a auspicious star to pass away, as told in sastras some additional rites have to be done. To them charities as oil, cow, ghee and hiranyam has to be done. If it is not done properly even the kartha who does rites will also get troubled.

For Shardha done for the pretha, certain acts normally done for other shradam need not be done. They are acts like blessings invoked from Brahmins, to enquire about the wellbeing of the person eating food, to do homa, to take care that dogs don't eat the food remains and to repeat swaha word and calling piturs after the food is served is not necessary. Also no need to do avaha and namaskarams or to go around the person eating food as pradhakshana.

Neither it is necessary to wear the sacred thread as per tradition. Also no need to do purnahathis in fire and ekothishtam.

Garuda! As soon as a person dies his hands and legs have to be tied. All the relations should stay near the body.

If a dead body is lying in a village all members of the village should not eat food or drink water. If they eat food it will be equivalent to eating meat and if they drink water it will be equivalent to the dosha of drinking blood.

They should not eat betel leaves and when the dead body is lying the couples should not unite and enjoy.

PRAYOPAVESAM, PILIGRIMAGE AND WORDLY LIFE

Garuda Bhagawan gave his respects to Parama padanathan and told `My blessed one! What is meant by doing Prayapavesam? How it became an important kriya?

If a person leaves his birth and living place and goes to a holy place and dies, what will be the gains for the person by that act? If a person dies during any pilgrimages what will happen to him later? What will a person get by doing regular pilgrimages? If a person takes sanyas ashram but later digresses from its rules what is the punishment he gets due to that?

Please explain all these to this humble one, thus Garuda entreated.

The paramapada nadan was highly pleased by this request and started telling Vinadeya! Whoever lives and dies in a discipline manner and while dying lies in the mat made of darpa grass and meditates on me, is sure to reach my abode.

Whoever does prayopavesam regularly, on each day he does it, it will be equivalent to doing a homa. By this act alone he will then realize the truth of this life and greatness of God behind all acts. Knowing these truths he will come to the conclusion that there is no need of this life and will do prayopavesam and reach a good world.

In case a person decides first that there is no need of this life and with a strong mind does prayopavesam, but at the last stage he changes his mind and enters again into the life process, then he must do `prayachitams"(redeeming) deeds with the help of Brahmins and follow strict dharmic path till the end of his life.

In case a person takes renunciation (sanyas) and follows the code very strictly till death, then right from the day of taking sanyas till death, each day two-homa benefits will reach him.

In case a person due to miseries in family life takes up sanyas and later as troubles in family ease out comes back and accepts family life, then he will be considered a great sinner and he has to bear the hardships. Such a turnaround is considered a great sin. It will be even sinful to interact with a papi of such an order.

If a person gets a determination and with viragya leaves his wife and children and others, goes on long pilgrimage, it will be looked kindly by the devas who will shower on him all good tidings. In case a person decides to go to a holy place, which is far away, and stay there till his life leaves the body, however on the way his life ebbs away, he will reach swarga.

The devas will protect the renounced sanyasa, in particular the Vishnu ganas will protect him.

If a person plans to die in holy place and stays there for long time but die due to some reason happens to die just when he is out of that place, then in next janma he will get born in a good vedic family, staying near a holy river who are well versed in sastras, who follow good conduct, who are bhaktis of bhagawan and bhagawan works. He will live a good life there, finally after the death in that janma will reach a good loka.

If a person decides that he will go to a holy place stay there till the end of his life and such a sankalp he takes in front of learned pandits near a water source then proceeds on his journey but breaks his own promise and returns to his home town, then he will be a great sinner. He has to do a number of prayachittam (redeeming acts) to come out of the sins.

After knowing the death time is nearing if a person decides he has to die in one of the Lord vishnu's holy places and undertakes a long journey, each step he takes is equal to giving in charity a cow. For any reason if such a person returns back home, then for every step he retraces are equal to killing a cow, such a dosha he will acquire.

The sins a person does in his family life can be washed off by visiting pilgrimage centers and doing service for god and taking prasadams of holy places. However if he does sins in holy places such sins will never be cleared by any means at any time.

Garuda! It is more important to help and take care of one's own father, mother, the brother and sisters born along with one than to help outsiders.

If a son takes care of his father and provides for his needs, these acts will fetch him hundred times more punya than giving to a good Brahmin.

Taking care and providing for mother will give him thousand times more punya. Taking care of one's sister is amounting to one lakh times more punya than any other person. Taking care of one's brother gets punya beyond any measure.

A person who has gathered wealth with pain and trouble should know to use and distribute it well.

Whoever is born, as a human being has to die one day or another? But forgetting this simple fact, persons take great care of his impermanent body, decorate it with beautiful clothes, get involved and get immersed in samsara sagara (worldly life).

Seeing such foolish jives Yama laughs and thinks `Indeed what is the brainpower of such human beings! Though he has obtained a human form which he carefully nourishes, is it not by his deeds he will get caught by me in my net and get evaluated".

Bhoo devi (goddess of mother earth) looking at a miser who though possessed with lot of wealth but does not use it on himself or give it to others will laugh at him thinking` Is this all really belongs to him.

This simple fact the foolish son of mine does not know. The land and all the wealth which he thinks as his does not belong to him. Persons who remain closed in with their property telling this is mine, I am the owner, finally even without calling a half-meter cloth as their own leave everything here and go to Yama lok.

That being the fate of the human beings what is the meaning in calling anything as their own.
Remaining with good character and keeping a good conduct, helping the fellow living being in proper time and doing different charities like land, cow will please bhoo devi.

She will think My good son, by him I am given in the hands of another good son of mine as charity' and she will become happy.

The person who has done bhu dhan (charity of land), the one who do penance and follow austerities, the one who does homa and yagnas, the one who stands steadfast in hi karma and do not run back even from battle fields and goes out boldly to even sacrifice his life will become blessed soul both here an in worlds above! Thus told Lord Tirumal.

XVI

THE WAYS TO GET SWARGA AND MOKSHA

Garuda bhagawan gave his humble pranams once again to Lord Sriman Narayana and addressed this `Jagadeesa! How to do daily sharda? Kindly explain it to me.'

For that the lord who is personification of everything dharmic looked at the king of birds and told, `Vinadeya! Every day a good Brahmin should be given food and then annam and `punal' should be filled in a pot and the Brahmin should be given this as a charity.

In this way if nitya (daily) shradh is done then the dead person will become happy. The Yama kingaras who accompany the jive for one year, walking along with the jive to Yamapuri will also become happy.

Because of this act they will treat the jive properly. On the 12th day taking `sankalp' for the dead person, twelve pots have to be given on charity. If he had been poverty stricken a big pot should be given in name of Lord Vishnu and a pot should be given in name of Chitragupta, thus told Lord Tirumal.

Hearing that Garuda gave his pranams to Him and further asked Him` Parama padanatha! By dying in which holy place a jive can expect to get moksha (relieved from the cycle of birth and death) and swarga.

By doing what karmas these two can be obtained? Kindly tell me that and bless this humble one. Sri Vaikuntanathan perumal looked at Garuda and told `Ayodhya, Mathura, Gaya, Kasi, Avanthika, Dwaraka, these are the holy cities where a person leaving his life will reach the blessed abode of Vaikunta.

Also persons who take sanyasa and dies, one who is a ardent Vishnu bhaktha, one who keeps repeating Lord Rama and Lord Krishan's name and dies will also reach swarga.

A person who comes forward to forsake one's life when small children, Brahmins and cow come to danger in order to protect them will also be welcomed in swarga by all devas.

There are other holy places which also merit mention. They are Srirangam, Kasi, Kurukshetra, Bhrigushetra, Prabhasa thirtham, kanchi, Pushkaram, Bhudeshwaram etc. Persons who meet their end at these places too are considered meritorious.

Charities like land, house, cow, and elephant are considered meritorious and such persons will reach swarga after death.

Persons who get involved in renovation work of water bodies like well, canal, pond and temples will fetch even more punya than the persons who originally made it.

Also persons who have done Vrishorsargam regularly will also reach swarga, thus told Lord Tirumal.

POLLUTION – Aasousam

Listen Oh! Great saints, As soon as Paramatma told Garuda about the daily shardha and about the importance of pilgrimage to holy places, Lord Garuda looked at Bhagawan and asked `Sarvesa, what is meant by Aasousam (pollution), please tell me about this in detail' thus he entreated.

The Aadhi Narayana started telling Garuda thus, oh! Vinadeya! If a child is born or a child is dead, for his clan people (dayadhis) ten days Aasousam is there. Persons who are afflicted with pollution should not do homas and puja related works. Till the pollution gets over others should not take food in that particular house.

For persons who have met unnatural death like falling in a fire and meeting death, getting killed by wild animals, going to far off places and dying there, for these people karmas should not be done immediately. Only when the rites get started his family people and clan persons will have pollution.

As soon as one hears a person is dead one should take bath
For the king, for the ascetic who does penance and for a great Brahmin who does big yagnas there is no pollution even if their clan people die.

If a person gets a girl child his clan people does not have pollution. Only the mother has 10 days pollution. For the father of the child only a bath is required to get out of pollution.

If a person is about to get married or a person is about to conduct yagna or if a person is getting ready for a big festivity, that time he hears the news of some one of his dayadhi's birth or death that at such a time there is no pollution till he finishes the job in hand.

If any charity is planned before knowing about pollution than that charity can be done after the pollution.

If a person meets the death when protecting cows, women or Brahmin then persons around him have to observe pollution only for a day.

There are also people who tell it is enough to take bath and for such persons there is no pollution to be observed at all.

RESULTS OF MEETING A BAD DEATH

Garuda looked at Lord Perumal and addressed him `Oh! Protector of the entire world! Tell me what is the fate of a jive, which meets its death in a bad manner? What sort of rites has to be done to him? Please tell me that ' thus he requested.

The husband of Goddess Lakshmi, Sri Hari started telling thus-

Garuda! The one who dies by hanging by taking poison by fire by taking powdered diamond or is struck by beak of birds, hit by a bull or falls in the water and is drowned or bit by wild animals or dogs or bit by poisonous snake or other poisonous insects or killed by other human beings, hit by thunder bolt or meets death due to a tree falling on him, such kind of death which happens in a unfortunate manner are not considered a good death.

Such a jive after death will not reach a good state. It will reach hell. For such a death the near one's have no pollution. There is no need to do rites for them immediately. Only after doing Narayana Bali the rites have to be done.

For a person who meets a bad death if he is a Brahmin the rites have to be performed after six months, if he is a Khastriya after two months, if he is a Vaisya after 15teen days and if he is a sudra as soon as he dies.

It is a must to do Narayana bali either in the banks of Ganges or banks of Yamuna or in Narmada or pushkara Keshtra or at least under the shade of a Banyan tree or in cow shed or in the house itself.

God has to be worshipped by telling veda mantras then by sitting south facing the Lord Narayana has to be addressed and prayed thus, Oh! Swami, you have worn the conch shell, chakra and yellow garments, who is ever present, who is found everywhere.

whose form is all encompassing, who is personification of happiness, bearer of all tidings, I entreat you to lead the dead person to a good state, thus praying to the Lord and meditating on his blessed form with lot of bhakti the Brahmins have to be fed, they should be given wealth and food as charity and pinda dhanam and tharpanam should be done.

After doing these the next day an idol made up of gold of Sri Vishnu, an idol made of copper of Lord rudra an idol made of silver of Lord Brahma an idol made up of iron of Lord Yama has to be made.

Lord Vishnus idol should be kept in west, Lord Brahma's idol should be kept in east, in south Lord Yamas, in north Lord rudra's idol to be kept, in the middle the dead persons idol has to be kept and worshipped.

Along with that five kumbas (pots filled with water with coconut kept over it) have to be kept. In that Navarathnas have to be inserted and the same to be decorated with sacred threads and the above five devas shradha has to be done, then pindas have to be kept for them. Eight types of dhanas have to be done.

In a copper vessel oil and hiranyam have to be kept and done charity. Then for the one who chants the Vedas, a feroile land has to be given as charity. For the one who chants Yajur veda a cow along with a calf has to be given for the one who chants sama veda sambha paddy has to be given.

Then collecting 360 stalks of jack fruit tree leaves, the dead persons idol should be done.

Garuda! I will tell you the reasons and significance for 360 stalks.
For head forty, for neck 10, for chest 20, for stomach 20, for things 100, for knees 30 for sex organs four for legs ten.

Then for head a coconut, for face five ratnas for tongue a banana fruit, for nose a flower named `etti' for ear oil for nerves stalk of lotus flower for muscle Annam for blood honey for hair false hair set for skin krishnajinam for breast `kuntri' for navel lotus flower has to be kept.

Then the place has to be decorated with sandalwood and flowers and in a sastric way rites have to be performed.

If things are done in this manner a person who has met an unfortunate death will reach a good state. A son who does karma like this will have 10-day pollution and other clan persons (dayadhis) will have three-day pollution.

XVII

KAMIA VRIKSHOSARGAM

The sarvajan god Narayana looked at Garuda and started telling ` Vainadeya, I will tell you about a special Vrikshorsargam'

On one of the days when doing the rites after cleaning the place where the rites are to be conducted and after installing the agni (fire), same color calves, one male calf slightly big and a female calf slightly small has to be brought in.

They should be given bath by yellow turmeric water decorated with clothes and ornaments. Then tarpana should be done and they should be let off. Then a nandhi shradahm should be done and for 15teen days food has to be served for Brahmins. Further silver, oil, udhaka kumbha, clothes etc has to be given on charity.

By doing so 101 generation of one's lineage people will reach heaven. This is called Kamia Vrishorsargam.

THE REASONS FOR HAPPINESS AND SORROW.

THE BENEFITS ACCRUED BY CHARITY.

Vinadeya! The reason a jive obtains happiness and sorrow before death and after death are all due to the good and bad deeds done by the jive.

Though there are multitudes of jives how is it possible for each and every action to reach the correct doer in the next janma? This doubt you may get but really there should not be any doubt about it.

Even though in one place a lot of cows in large groups are grazing till a calf left in the group will reach its mother without fail. Same way the karmas also will reach a particular person responsible for it without fail.

Vainadeya! There is no charity above doing budhana (charity of land). There is no goodness or punya act above telling the truth. There is no sin greater than telling lies and writing false documents.

As earth (bhumi) is related to Lord Vishnu as he has taken in marriage budevis daughter and cows are the daughters of Lord sun while gold is the son of Lord agni, thus by giving on charity these three things a person will reap lot of benefits by these charities.

If a person gives charity of land but later with greed or covertness tries to get back the land then the person who helps him in this act and the person who does such a retracing act all will reach naraka and will remain there Till pralya period.

If a person is doing a job and living and if another person is the cause to destroy his job than the second person will collect the sins as of killing of thousand cows.

At the same time if a person helps another in getting a livelihood then he will reap benefit of one l lakh godhan.

However instead of during charity of hundred cows it is better not to torture one cow by beating it with stick or not to steal one cow. If a person kills one cow and does charity of hundred cows he will be getting the sin of killing one cow more strongly.

If charity is given to an exalted well-disciplined Brahmin who has learned all four Vedas and help him in such a way that he has not to worry about his daily living than such a charity will be equal to doing an ashvameda yagna.

If a king snatches the wealth of Brahmins and with that wealth collects an army. Then with such an army he wages a war, that army will meet its end in the war for sure.

If a person takes back a charity given to a person doing holy deeds like yagna, homa, chanting of hymns, than it amounts to a great sin such an act should never be done.

On doing such an act, the person will be born as a lowly germ in stools for thousand hundred years and remain there itself.

If a person is coveting on some things and makes false friendship with good Brahmins and takes away their things then he will rot in hell for long time.

It is even possible to digest rock powder, iron powder or even poison. However for stealing and digesting a Brahmins thing there is no place in all three worlds.

A person who steals god's jewels and other things, the one who snatches things from good men and the one who condemns and insults persons who are involved in doing holy work, such persons lineage will get destroyed.

However there is no merit in giving to a not so deserving Brahmin charity. It is like doing `ahuthi' to ash. During punya days like sankranthi if dhana and dharmas are done than sun god will increase the bounties of the giver limitless extent.

A Brahmin who is stickler to his daily discipline, who has not a bit digressed from his brahminic disciplines who does not partake food at any outside places for such a Brahmin even if a land covered with sea is given as charity, he won't pick up any dosha for accepting charities but the giver of charity will be bestowed with special blessings.

CHILDRENS PAPAS AND TARPANAS TO UNFORTUNATE.

Vasudeva started once again telling to Garuda who is Vinudha's son `Vinadeya! From four years to twelve years, whatever papa's children do will get attached to the parents only? If parents are not there than it will belong to the guardians.

The parents should do compensation (prayachit) for these acts. For children who do papa, the sins won't get attached. They should not be punished by the state too.

A person who is affected by disease in case he is not able to take bath during pollution, than a person who is not having pollution can touch him and do `patravarthi bath, than the first person's pollution will get removed.

TARPANAS TO UNFORTUNATE SOULS

Whoever is sticking to concepts like there is no god will be a big sinner. For him and for persons who meet unfortunate deaths there is no need to do rites.

If a yagna is done for them then the agni can be thrown in water and aupashanas can be thrown in the middle of four streets. However when the year is getting over with compassion his son can worship Lord Vishnu and lord Yama during sukla paksha ekadasi, thinking about the dead person ten pindas can be made and offered in a nearby river or water spot, then facing southwards the dead person's name has to be told three times.

Later bath has to be taken and one has to remain upvas (abstaining from food). Then next day invite five to seven Brahmins well versed in vedas and make them sit in wooden seats facing north and praying to Lord Vishnu those Brahmins have to be fed well.

Then five pinda has to be kept in name of SriVishnu, Brahma, Shiva, and Lord Yama along with his duthas and the dead person. Then the dead person's name and gotra has to be told and Sri Vishnus names to be chanted.

Since the dead person cannot join with the ancestors, his pinda the fifth one has to be removed. Then pranams has to be done to the gods and charities to be given and the five Brahmins have to be given dakshina (money) for eating food.

The Brahmin who represents the dead person should be given more dakshina and one has to pray to Lord Vishnu that He should get satisfied and bless. Then those Brahmins have to be given namaskarams doing prathakshina to them, and then facing south tarpana has to be done.

If the son wants to do till in an elaborate manner he can do a snake form in gold and then do the rites as told above.

XVIII

SHARDH TO BE DONE DAILY THROUGH THE YEAR

Bhagawan who is complete with six qualities looked at Garuda and started telling

`Son of kashipa! A son should do shradha to one's parents every year. If a situation arises that a father has to do shradha to his son or a brother to his younger brother than while doing shradha the ancestors name should not be taken, only the dead person's name the shradha has to be done.

If pollution (Aasousam) happen to fall on shradha days then only after they are over the rites has to be done.

If monthly shradha is being done to a dead person and if for that person sapandikaranam is not done, in that situation if the masika gets stopped due to some pollution then that masika can be done combining with another masika.

If a person doing masika after doing sapandikaranam and a pollution (aasousam) falls in between then the halted masika can be done in the day when pollution gets removed.

If a son who has not worn sacred thread happens to do shradha that should be done after doing proper `sankalpa'.

If the news comes that many people of one's clan die at the same time in a far off place then who's ever death is known first, for him rites should be done and then the later heard persons rites should be done.

If the day or thidhi is known when death occurred but month of death is not known than rites can be done during Aadi, puratazi, margazi, mazi months in krishnapaksham or ashtami or during amavasa.

If a person's death is known at a far off place but if date and month of death is not known than the rites can be done on the day he started the journey.

If head of a family goes for a journey along with his relations that time if one of them passes away than the head of the family should observe pollution there itself and then only venture home.

In case one forgets the date of fathers, mother's death anniversary then shradh can be done during ashtami or Ekadasi or amavasi. However instead of doing on an alternate day if the shradh is left out then it is a sinful act.

If a person does daily shradh till he dies every day, he will get lot of good tidings form it. This shradh is not done for the dead person but to the living person for his good then no Avahan to be done.

The Brahmin who eats in this shradh does not have to follow any particular rules. It is enough if daily food is given to a good Brahmin thus told Tirumal and blessed and further told, Garuda! I have answered all the questions asked by you, if you have any more question do come forth.

INDICATIONS OF GOOD AND BAD DEEDS OF PREVIOUS BIRTHS AND FUTURE BIRTHS

Garuda gave his respects to Sri Vasudevan. `Swami! Looking at the jives, who appear in this world, is it possible to tell this jive would have done such karma in previous birth just applying common sense.

Is there anyone other than Yama who punishes the jive for his misdeeds? You must kindly tell about these to this humble one in detail.

For that the Prandama looked at the Bhakti Garuda and told, `Oh! Son of Kasipa muni! It can be clearly known that this jive has this papa (sin) or this punya (good deed)

If a student does mistake his teacher punishes him. If he is an evil person and not coming under the control of the teacher or guardian than he will be punished by the king or state.

If he is an evildoer but does sins without anyone knowing then he will be well punished by Yama. If a person doing papa dies without doing any prayachita (redeeming acts) for the papa done then he will remain in hell (narak) for long time and get born as a low jive like a dog, wolf or other animals, then later on he may get a human beings birth.

He may also get born with certain character and marks, which reveals the papas done by him in previous birth.

If a person is seen with difficulty in talking forth, having chest pain and difficulty in speech then it can be known he must have in previous janma told lot of lies and must have stayed in narak.

A person who had kept fire for another person's house or who had killed and murdered other human beings may suffer from `kushtarog'. The one who drinks in the afternoon time may get teeth like small insects.

One who gets work in low places can be guilty in stealing gold.

A person who gets an ugly form can be the one who had tried to seduce one's own teacher's wife.

A poverty stricken person would have been guilty of being a miser and not shared his wealth with others. If many pandits are there in a village and one pandit only commits a sin, till all the pandits in the village will be tainted by the sin.

A person who takes food without taking bath without doing sandhya vandanam or worshipping, he will get the birth of a crow. A person who takes food in the open instead of under a shelter or inside the house will be born as a black monkey in a deserted place in the next janma.

A person who shouts and scolds others without proper reason will be born as a cat. A person who burns trees will get a life of a firefly. Persons who had fed others with things that are not good for them and also persons who had enjoyed with women other than wedded one will be born as bull that pulls load.

Persons who had given old food to the one who do yagnas will get the life of black monkey. A person who has been hostile to others and shouted at others for no reason will be born blind.

Persons who have robbed books will become blind sometime after he is born. A person who had brought destruction of a Brahmin family will loose his children as soon as they are born.

Persons who had denied food to others when they are hungry will be bereft of childbirth. Persons who had stolen cloth will get the life of a leech. Persons who had given poison to kill others will be born as snake.

A person who enjoyed with a lady whose husband had taken renunciation will get the janma of a ghost. Persons who had enjoyed with other women will meet an early death. Persons who coveted for his teacher's wife will get the life of a lizard.

Persons who cover the public land of a well or pond to make use of it for own purpose will be born as a fish. A person who has acted against the judgment given to him will become a `kottan'. The one who has eaten in ekodihsta food will get birth of a jackal.

Persons who had insulted higher caste people will get the birth of a tortoise. A person who cuts trees filled with flowers and fruits will be condemned as a worthless person.

Persons who steal scented objects will be born as a foul smelling person. Stealing is a heinous crime. Persons who steal others things will definitely get a very low birth.

I have previously itself told about the Vitharani river found in the way to Yamaloka filled with blood, pus and various strange animals and crocodiles. In that river like a molten butter the dirt will be flowing. For persons who have done very heinous crime that river is the only one to take bath.

Persons who are full of self-pride and ego, one's who had insulted their own parents, teacher and elders one who had failed to respect the person who had helped him at time of need, one's who treat women, children with least respect, one's who heckle and make fun of the handicapped persons like deaf, dumb and others, one's who have acted with hostility in marriage matters and Brahmins matters, one's who had promised he will give some charities but later makes the recipient walk several times to get the charity, one who forms illicit relationship with one's own teachers wife, one's who show disrespect in places where religious discourse and other religious activities take place by talking loudly other worldly matters, one who talk badly and spread rumour about the girl whose marriage alliance is being proposed , one who fail to take care of cow and other domestic animals under his care or show partiality while taking care of other persons domestic animal, ones who give some article willingly to another but later covet for it and wish to have it back, one's who argue heatedly that god is not there, one's who always show anger to others and blame others constantly will all get drowned in the Vaitharani river and will be troubled by strange animals , crocodiles and other beings staying in the water.

Vainadeya! The jives who have not done bad deeds but always have concentrated doing good deeds will after death reach swarga and remain there for some time, then later will be born at a good place in an exalted family and will be endowed with knowledge of all sastras and get wealth for doing a good living and will lead a good life.

When father dies and before the son is out of pollution, if the son hears this purana than the father will reach the blessed abode of Myself at Vaikunta.

If when mother dies this purana is heard than that mother will get a man's janma, live a good life and reach swarga.

The piturs also will reach a good state. If this purana is read during sankranthi, on Vishu (the new year day) during grahana (eclipse) time during shradha days, then such people at the end of one' life will reach a good world.

The good benefit received from one crore kanya dhanams, hundred times doing sodasa mahadhan, doing gaya shradha are all obtained by making people read this purna and making people hear this purana.

To make jives get rid of fear of yamalok and to make jives aware of the path to moksha (liberation), I am telling you this purana. Also for the benefit of goodness of the entire world, thus Lord Tirumal and blessed Garuda.

Then Garuda gave his grateful thanks to the most compassionate, most considerate bhagawan Lord Narayana and went around him, fell on his lotus feet and spoke with great emotion and humility `Oh! Lord you are the one who taught Vedam to veda itself by the same blessed tongue I was graced to hear this purana, it is indeed my fortune, what penance I must have done to hear this purana,

SARVE JANA SUKUNO BAVANTHU LOKHA SAMASTHA SAMAGALA BAVANTHU

Thus that Suuthamuni told this purana to Naimacharanya munis and then addressing them further told,
`Respected Munis! As you wanted to hear this purana, I told you all exactly the same way as it was narrated to Garuda by Lord Narayana' thus telling he started singing Hari's name, praising the Lord.

That time the Naimicharanya residents hearing that purana were immersed in a sea of happiness and looked at Suuthamuni and told ` Oh! Great muni! Taking compassion on us you told us this purana.

We have of course heard lot of puranas told by you. This purana in particular gives the jive a firmness and support for the life he is leading in this bhulok. We want to honour you and show our gratitude to you.

Such a thought is very strong with all of us. However we are not endowed with great wealth, you are very much aware of our state,
From the group one of them got up and offered his armlet to Suutha muni to show his gratitude, another one presented a dress made of bark, yet another gave a skin of tiger for Suutha muni to sit, one of them gave the sacred thread as gift, while one of them wondering what to give, gave the darpa grass as the present.

While one praised the Suutha muni telling ` Is there any one as great as Suutha muni in the three worlds who can narrate purans like this. Another one gave his humble pranams several times and showed his gratitude. Then all of them went around Suutha muni in respect giving him their pranams and departed to their respective ashrams.

Sarve jana sukuno bavanthu loka samtha samgala bavanthu

The Garuda Purana is one of the 18 Puranas composed by **Ved Vyasa** in order to explain Vedic principles. It was in a forest called Naimisha, where the narration happened for the first time.

Authors Bio:

T. Krishna Dinesh is a Management Graduate who specialises in human relations.

Being brought up in a traditional background family he developed a sense of interest in the purana gadhas told by his grandparents.

This is an attempt to rekindle the stories all alike for those whether they had the privilege or not in their childhood.

Please write to booklove788@gmail.com for feedback & suggestions